THE
CONDITIONAL
PROMISES
OF
GOD

THE
CONDITIONAL
PROMISES
OF
GOD

Dominic M. Esposito

TATE PUBLISHING & *Enterprises*

Published by Tate Publishing & Enterprises, LLC
127 E. Trade Center Terrace | Mustang, Oklahoma 73064 USA
1.888.361.9473 | www.tatepublishing.com

Tate Publishing is committed to excellence in the publishing industry. The company reflects the philosophy established by the founders, based on Psalm 68:11,
"The Lord gave the word and great was the company of those who published it."

Book design copyright © 2009 by Tate Publishing, LLC. All rights reserved.
Cover design by Jeff Fisher
Interior design by Stefanie Rooney

Published in the United States of America

ISBN: 978-1-60799-591-3
1. Religion, Christian Life, Devotional
2. Religion, Biblical Studies, Bible Study Guides
09.09.01

The Conditional Promises of God
Being Doers of the Word and Not Hearers Only

Condensed Edition

Editor*: Christy Marsh Haines*
Editorial Assistant: *Kathy Durkee*

For information contact:

Dominic M. Esposito
www.TheConditionalPromisesOfGod.org

—— I thankfully dedicate this work to ——

My Lord and Savior
Jesus Christ

My loving and faithful bride
Linda

My precious daughters
Salina and Alicia

My Pa-Pa, pastor, mentor, and friend
Dr. Amar B. Rambisoon

My dear brother in Christ
Dennis Fuller

My dearest family and friends who have long
supported this labor of love since 1996

And to all—throughout the world—
who will be called and reached—
through the power of His true Word—
*to be doers of the Word
and not hearers only*

Table of Contents

The Conditional Promises are grouped into
various Life Topics, and *numbered in the
order they were discovered in the Bible.*

NOTE: Since this book is the *Condensed Edition* of *The Conditional Promises of God*, not all of the conditional promises of God regarding His blessings are printed in their expanded form, as they are in the *Unabridged Edition. Note that Life Topics 1 and 14 are omitted from the Condensed Edition, and are found in their entirety in the Unabridged Edition.*

The Unabridged Edition is available from
www.TheConditionalPromisesOfGod.org.

Foreword

There are almost thirty-seven hundred Conditional Promises of God encompassed in thirty-three practical Life Topics in His Word.

Only one of those thirty-three topics is for the person who has *not* believed in his heart by faith, and confessed with his mouth the Lord Jesus Christ as his Savior.

> But what does it say? "The word is near you, in your mouth and in your heart" (that is, the word of faith which we preach): that if you *confess with your mouth the Lord Jesus and believe in your heart* that God has raised Him from the dead, *you will be saved.* For with the heart one believes unto righteousness, and with the mouth confession is made unto salvation. For the Scripture says, "Whoever believes on Him will not be put to shame." For there is no distinction between Jew and Greek, for the same Lord over all is rich to all who call upon Him. For "whoever calls on the name of the Lord shall be saved."
>
> Romans 10:8–13

The other thirty-two topics are for those individuals who *have* professed their faith in the Lord Jesus Christ for their hope in eternal life with Christ. In order for someone to become a "doer of the word," and therefore be eligible to receive the benefits of the "positive/blessing" Conditional Promises of God—he needs to be a child of God, that is, a born-again Christian.

But even Christians are not taking advantage of the great many blessings available to them, because they are not aware of them, and therefore are not participating in the riches of God's promises to them.

Introduction

This is not a "name it and claim it" book. God is not a genie in a bottle, or in this case, the Bible. This is where it all comes down to the passion of the love relationship between the bride (you, the Church), and her husband (Jesus Christ, the Lord our God).

Therefore, the conditions outlined in a Conditional Promise of God should be the very things we *desire* to do—because they are what *please* God. We *don't* do them for what we can *get* from Him. We *do* them because we *love* Him, and want to *please* Him.

The fact that God has revealed how He desires to respond to what we do that pleases Him, serves to make the intimacy in the relationship that much more personal.

The timeliness and timelessness of this work—for defining clarity of boundaries, working out our own salvation, walking in love as imitators of God, and being lights in the ever-increasing darkness of this world—has never been greater. And its vision and purpose reaches across all mankind, answering the question, *"Why did God create Conditional Promises?"*

God created His Conditional Promises—

To call, reach, and teach unsaved persons about His Conditional Promises, which are, except for one of them, only for people who have made a choice to believe on Jesus Christ to be their personal Savior/Messiah.

To reach both the backslider and the wavering, unfruitful believer, whose desire is to return to the cross and live the life of abundance, which Jesus promises to the doer of the Word.

To encourage the believer, who feels he is right with God, but who has no real idea how few of God's Conditional Promises he has appropriated for himself, because he has not really understood what his part is in this relationship. This group is called to become *rededicated* doers of the Word and not hearers only.

To equip church leadership with a tool to lead its "pew-warming members" into active service for reaching the lost, and edifying the body.

To enable youth to become the true strike force of today and tomorrow; to face and overcome any temptation; and to become examples of encouragement to others who are facing adversity, hardships, and temptations; pointing them to the Way, to true success in life through Jesus Christ.

Dominic M. Esposito, Th.D

Small Beginnings

On May 5, 1996, I took the first step on a journey that I had never envisioned. I called my friend, Dennis Fuller, who was living in Anchorage, Alaska. He was sharing with me how the fourth chapter of Romans had been a blessing to him. He had been reading it over and over for days, and God was both ministering to him and directing his life through it. Because he had found comfort and encouragement, I decided to spend some time studying the first four chapters of Romans and see what God might show me. Little did I know that God was planting the seeds that have become the book that you are holding in your hand.

After two weeks of studying in the fourth chapter of Romans, God spoke to me within the consciousness of my spirit as clear as a bell. Layer by layer was unfolded within. I became more revived by the hour. The revival centered on this verse:

"He did not waver at the promises of God through unbelief, but was strengthened in faith, giving glory to God, and being fully convinced that what He had promised He was also able to perform. And therefore, *it* was accounted to him for righteousness" (Romans 4:20–22, NKJV).

The Scriptures say *"it"* was accounted to him for righteousness. But what was the *"it"* that was accounted to him for righteousness? If most Christians were asked what the *"it"* is referring to, they would say his faith. I thought so too at first. However, after a closer study, I determined that his faith alone was not what the *"it"* is. Look closer and let's reason together.

1. *"He* did not waver at the promises of God through unbelief."
   Who did this, God or Abraham?

2. *"He* was strengthened in faith."
   Who did this, God or Abraham?

3. *"He* gave glory to God."
   Who did this, God or *Abraham?*

4. *"He* was fully convinced that what God promised, He was also able to perform."
   Again, *Abraham* did this, not God.

And therefore…"it" was accounted to him for righteousness.

The *"it"* is the *combination of the four things that Abraham did.* Abraham did all these things *(not God)* because of his faith. The Bible tells us that faith without works is dead, and that we are justified by works, and not by faith only. Read this in the New Testament book of James (2:14–26), which was written by the half-brother of Jesus.

It was then that I was determined to know—what promises did God have waiting for me in His Word? It took me the next seven years to discover them all.

Types of Promises

Throughout the Bible, there are *two types of promises*: *Unconditional Promises* and *Conditional Promises*. Examples of *Unconditional Promises* are when God says, "He makes His sun rise on the evil and on the good, and sends rain on the just and on the unjust" (Matthew 5:45, NKJV). Another promise is that the rainbow is a sign of His promise that He will never again destroy the earth by flood (Genesis 9:12–17). A person can claim unconditional promises of God if he likes, but God has already obligated Himself to fulfill those promises; the fact is they are not based on any pending conditions or special presupposed relationship.

The *Conditional Promises* of God are exemplified in the following examples.

> "Draw near to God and He will draw near to you."
> James 4:8 (NKJV)

The most important words in understanding this Conditional Promise are, "Draw near to God." God stands ready to draw near to us *if* we first draw near to God. *If* we do not draw near to God, He is not obligated to fulfill the part He's promised, namely that He will draw near to us.

Another Conditional Promise of God says to:

> "Trust in the Lord with all your heart, and lean not on your own understanding; in all your ways acknowledge Him, and He shall direct your paths."
> Proverbs 3:5–6 (NKJV)

God has promised to direct our paths. What a great promise! Look again! First we have to 1) put our total trust in Him; 2) not depend on our own intellect and logic; and 3) in every way (acting, talking, thinking) we must recognize God in it, by it, and through it. Only *then,* God says, will He direct our paths. *These are called the Conditional Promises of God.*

Next, God unfolded the deep meanings of James 1:22–25, and James 2:14–26, to lead me to understand that my works are *because* of my faith. It opened by telling me to be a doer of the word and not a hearer only. It concluded with the fact that, just as the body without the spirit is dead, so faith without works is dead also.

I encourage you to take the time to read this text in its entirety.

We are required *To Be Doers of the Word and Not Hearers Only*—in doing so, we will be blessed. How will we be blessed—*through the blessings of God's Conditional Promises.* In order to receive God's Conditional Promises, we must first meet God's conditions by putting our faith into obedient actions—and then God is freed to fulfill his Conditional Promises, according to His will, time, and purposes.

When teaching, I ask Christians to take out a sheet of paper and write down any ten of God's Conditional Promises, where they are found in the Bible, and what conditions the doer of the Word must do as his part in the relationship. All too often this is a very difficult assignment to complete.

By May 16, only eleven days after talking with Dennis, the course was set before me, and I prayerfully launched into the work God had revealed and directed. On that morning, I began a deep, diligent search for God's Conditional Promises—beginning at the very beginning—Genesis 1:1.

I quickly discovered that *God often makes more than*

one promise, or requires more than one condition within the context of a Conditional Promise. Also, God *does not always neatly package every promise with its conditions in one single verse.* Often the promises are spread throughout two or more verses, and many times the conditions are found before, within, and even after His Conditional Promises.

Going back to the earlier example, this is a Conditional Promise that is contained is a single verse.

"Draw near to God *and* He will draw near to you" (James 4:8, NKJV).

Conversely the next Conditional Promise example is spread out over two verses in Proverbs 3:5–6. And this example has one Conditional Promise, and three responsibilities of the Doer of the Word.

1. Trust in the Lord with all your heart,
2. And lean not on your own understanding,
3. In all your ways acknowledge Him,
    … and He shall direct your paths.

Once your heart and eyes become open to seeing the *Conditional Promises of God*, the Holy Spirit will cause them to jump off the pages, and you will never read Scripture in the same way again.

There is something else to understand about God's Conditional Promises in the Bible. God's Conditional Promises encourage, bless, reward, train, and build up His children in ways today's society would call "positive" blessings. God's Conditional Promises also include curses, punishment, destruction, and even death, in what today's society would deem "negative and cruel." This book of *The Conditional Promises of God* only reveals those Conditional Promises that bring out the positive blessings that can be received.

The Names and Order of All the Books of the Old and New Testaments with their Abbreviations

THE BOOKS OF THE OLD TESTAMENT

Book	Abbr.	Book	Abbr.
Genesis	Gen.	Ecclesiastes	Eccl.
Exodus	Ex.	The Song of Solomon	Song
Leviticus	Lev.	Isaiah	Isa.
Numbers	Num.	Jeremiah	Jer.
Deuteronomy	Deut.	Lamentations	Lam.
Joshua	Josh.	Ezekiel	Ezek.
Judges	Judg.	Daniel	Dan.
Ruth	Ruth	Hosea	Hos.
1 Samuel	1 Sam.	Joel	Joel
2 Samuel	2 Sam.	Amos	Amos
1 Kings	1 Kgs.	Obadiah	Obad.
2 Kings	2 Kgs.	Jonah	Jon.
1 Chronicles	1 Chron.	Micah	Mic.
2 Chronicles	2 Chron.	Nahum	Nah.
Ezra	Ezra	Habakkuk	Hab.
Nehemiah	Neh.	Zephaniah	Zeph.
Esther	Esth.	Haggai	Hag.
Job	Job	Zechariah	Zech.
Psalms	Ps.	Malachi	Mal.
Proverbs	Prov.		

THE BOOKS OF THE NEW TESTAMENT

Book	Abbr.	Book	Abbr.
Matthew	Matt.	1 Timothy	1 Tim.
Mark	Mark	2 Timothy	2 Tim.
Luke	Luke	Titus	Titus
John	John	Philemon	Philem.
Acts	Acts	Hebrews	Heb.
Romans	Rom.	James	James
1 Corinthians	1 Cor.	1 Peter	1 Pet.
2 Corinthians	2 Cor.	2 Peter	2 Pet.
Galatians	Gal.	1 John	1 John
Ephesians	Eph.	2 John	2 John
Philippians	Phil.	3 John	3 John
Colossians	Col.	Jude	Jude
1 Thessalonians	1 Thess.	Revelation	Rev.
2 Thessalonians	2 Thess.		

This is a sample of how to navigate through the pages that follow.

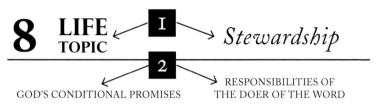

8 LIFE TOPIC → *Stewardship*

2

GOD'S CONDITIONAL PROMISES   RESPONSIBILITIES OF
                                   THE DOER OF THE WORD

1) Prov 10:4,5	Prov 10:4,5
4 ...the hand of... ...makes rich 5 He who ...is a wise son **3**	4 ...(of) the diligent (makes...) 5 ...(who) gathers in the summer (is...)
2) Prov 12:14	Prov 12:14
14 ...A man will be satisfied With good by... ...the recompense of... ...will be rendered to him	14 ...(by) the fruit of his mouth ...(of) a man's hand (will...)
3) Prov 28:25	Prov 28:25
25 ...he who... **4** ...will be prospered	25 ...(who) trusts in the Lord (will...)
65.4) Heb 7:8	Heb 7:8
8 ...but there he **5** receives them	8 Here mortal men receive tithes (but there...) **6**
Symbolic Commentary	
Melchizedek, a priest to whom Abraham gave his tithe, was without father or mother, having neither beginning nor end. He is the symbolic representation of Christ, who is alive forevermore. When the Doer of the Word gives in obedience, he is demonstrating his belief that God is alive and that the tithes he gives to mortal men (churches and ministries) will be received by God as if they had been given to Him directly.	

— How to Use this Reference Work —

I   The Conditional Promises of God Life Topic Titles are at the top of each page.

2   GOD'S CONDITIONAL PROMISES are on the left column of each page and the RESPONSIBILITIES OF THE DOER OF THE WORD are on the right column of each page.

3   As the lines descend from top to bottom, the verses flow from side to side connecting the Conditional Promises and the Doer of the Word's Responsibilities.

4   Each Conditional Promise of God is numbered as found in the unabridged edition. The book, chapter, and verse references match the *Index* listings.

5   Verse reference numbers indicate the Bible scripture being identified.

6   At the end of each *symbolic conditional promise* are practical application commentaries.

7   Use The Conditional Promises of God with your Bible. Highlight, memorize, and live them.

Important

These Conditional Promises of God have been extracted from their complete verses in the Bible. *In all cases, each Conditional Promise of God needs to be placed in its biblical context for a more complete understanding.*

THE
CONDITIONAL
PROMISES
OF
GOD

Condensed Edition

The chapters in this Condensed Edition are
arranged in topical order as discovered while
studying through the Bible in chronological order.

Topics one and fourteen do not have any
verses listed in this Condensed Edition.

LIFE TOPIC 1

Environment

Authority over the earth,
elements, and living creatures

Since this book is the *Condensed Edition* of *The Conditional Promises of God*, not all of the Conditional Promises of God regarding His blessings are printed in their expanded form, as they are in the *Unabridged Edition*. Life Topics 1 and 14 are omitted from the Condensed Edition, and are found in their entirety in the Unabridged Edition.

The Unabridged Edition is available from
www.TheConditionalPromisesOfGod.org.

LIFE TOPIC 2

Family

Relationship to spouse, children, and future generations

God's heart toward the family is expressed in how He desires family members to live for one another. The unity of family is best seen in how each family member benefits from his relationship with each of the other members — through love. If a man walks in a righteous way, his children will be blessed. When the children are grown and have not departed from the way of righteousness, they will in turn be a blessing to their parents.

12 Who is the man that fears the LORD? Him shall He teach in the way He chooses.

13 He himself shall dwell in prosperity, and his descendants shall inherit the earth.

14 The secret of the LORD is with those who fear Him ...

GOD'S CONDITIONAL PROMISES	RESPONSIBILITIES OF THE DOER OF THE WORD
3) Ps. 25:12, 13, 14	Ps. 25:12, 14
	12 ...the man that fears the LORD (Him...)
12 Him [the believer] shall He [God] teach in the way He chooses	
13 He himself shall dwell in prosperity [goodness] ...and his descendants shall inherit the earth	
14 The secret of the LORD is with those who...	14 ...(who) fear Him

There are four Conditional Promises God makes to us.

There are two responsibilities that we must do for God.

2 LIFE TOPIC *Family*

GOD'S CONDITIONAL PROMISES	RESPONSIBILITIES OF THE DOER OF THE WORD
3) Ps. 25:12, 13, 14	**Ps. 25:12, 14**
12 Him [the believer] shall He [God] teach in the way He chooses 13 He himself shall dwell in prosperity [goodness] ...and his descendants shall inherit the earth 14 The secret of the LORD is with those who...	12 ...the man that fears the LORD (Him...) 14 ...(who) fear Him
7) Ps. 128:3, 4, 6	**Ps. 128:4**
3 Your wife shall be like a fruitful vine in the very heart of your house ...your children like olive plants all around your table 4 Behold, thus shall the man be blessed who... 6 Yes, may you see your children's children	4 ...(who) fears the LORD
9) Prov. 20:7	**Prov. 20:7**
7 ...his children are blessed after him	7 The righteous man walks in his integrity (his...)

Family

LIFE TOPIC 2

GOD'S CONDITIONAL PROMISES	RESPONSIBILITIES OF THE DOER OF THE WORD
10) Prov. 22:6	Prov. 22:6
6 ...and when he (a child) is old he will not depart from it	6 Train up a child in the way he should go (and...)
12) Prov. 31:30	Prov. 31:30
30 Charm is deceitful and beauty is passing, but a woman who... ...she shall be praised	30 ...(who) fears the LORD (she...)
20) Col. 3:21	Col. 3:21
21 ...lest they become discouraged	21 ...Fathers, do not provoke your children (lest...)

LIFE TOPIC 3

Offerings

Of money, goods, time, and talents

God does not instruct us to pursue wealth or give our offerings as His way to raise money for religion — it is how God raises His children to learn to come to Him with the cares and desires of our hearts. The more of ourselves we trust to Him, the more He takes care of our needs. If we trust that He will take care of all of our needs, we feel peaceful about giving to those who are in need; God is honored, we are fulfilled, and are properly positioned to be blessed by God.

Psalm 112:1, 9

1 Blessed is the man who fears the LORD, who delights greatly in God's commandments.

9 He has dispersed abroad, he has given to the poor.

GOD'S CONDITIONAL PROMISES	RESPONSIBILITIES OF THE DOER OF THE WORD
3) Ps. 112:1	Ps. 112:1, 9
1 Blessed is the man who...	1 ...(who) fears the LORD ...(who) delights greatly in His commandments 9 ...(who) has dispersed abroad ...(who) has given to the poor

There is one Conditional Promise God makes to us.

There are four responsibilities that we must do for God.

3 LIFE TOPIC *Offerings*

GOD'S CONDITIONAL PROMISES	RESPONSIBILITIES OF THE DOER OF THE WORD
3) Ps. 112:1	**Ps. 112:1, 9**
1 Blessed is the man who...	1 ...(who) fears the LORD ...(who) delights greatly in His commandments 9 ...(who) has dispersed abroad ...(who) has given to the poor
4) Prov. 3:10	**Prov. 3:9**
10 ...so your barns will be filled with plenty [food, drink, and material goods] ...and (so) your vats [abilities, gifts, and talents] will overflow with new wine [anointing and spiritual power]	9 Honor the LORD with your possessions ...and (Honor the LORD) with the firstfruits of all your increase
5) Prov. 11:25	**Prov. 11:25**
25 ...will be made rich ...he who ...will also be watered himself	25 ...The generous soul (will...) ...(he who) waters (will...)
6) Prov. 14:21	**Prov. 14:21**
21 ...he who... ...happy is he	21 ...(who) has mercy on the poor (happy...)

Offerings

GOD'S CONDITIONAL PROMISES	RESPONSIBILITIES OF THE DOER OF THE WORD
7) Prov. 19:17	**Prov. 19:17**
17 He who… …lends to the LORD …and He will pay back what he has given	17 …(who) has pity [sympathy] on the poor (lends…)
8) Prov. 22:9	**Prov. 22:9**
9 He who… …will be blessed, for…	9 …(who) has a generous eye (will…) …(for) he gives of his bread to the poor
9) Prov. 28:27	**Prov. 28:27**
27 He who… …will not lack	27 …(who) gives to the poor (will…)
10) Isa. 32:8	**Isa. 32:8**
8 …a generous (noble minded, liberal or princely) man devises generous things, and by… 8 …he shall stand	8 …(by) [his] generosity [noble, liberality, or princeliness] (he…)

GOD'S CONDITIONAL PROMISES	RESPONSIBILITIES OF THE DOER OF THE WORD
11) Mal. 3:10, 11, 12	Mal. 3:10
	10 ...Bring all the tithes into the storehouse ...And try Me now in this (If...)
10 ...If I will not open for you the windows of heaven and pour out for you such blessing that there will not be room enough to receive it 11 And I will rebuke the devourer for your sakes, so that he will not destroy the fruit of your ground ...nor shall the vine fail to bear fruit for you in the field 12 ...and all nations [other believers] will call you blessed, for you will be a delightful land	

GOD'S CONDITIONAL PROMISES	RESPONSIBILITIES OF THE DOER OF THE WORD
13) Matt. 6:4	Matt. 6:1, 2, 3, 4
	1 ...do not do your charitable deeds before men, to be seen by them
	2 ...when you do a charitable deed, do not sound a trumpet before you...that they may have glory from men
	3 ...when you do a charitable deed, do not let your left hand know what your right hand is doing,
	4 that your charitable deed may be in secret (and...)
4 ...and your Father who sees in secret will Himself reward you openly	
14) Matt. 6:21	Matt. 6:20
	20 ...lay up for yourselves treasures in heaven
21 For where your treasure is, there your heart will be also	

GOD'S CONDITIONAL PROMISES	RESPONSIBILITIES OF THE DOER OF THE WORD
17) Luke 6:38	**Luke 6:38**
38 ...and it will be given to you: good measure ...pressed down ...shaken together ...running over will be put into your bosom For with the... ...it will be measured back to you	38 Give (and...) ...(the) same measure that you use (it...)
18) Luke 11:41	**Luke 11:41**
41 ...then indeed all things are clean to you	41 ...give alms of such things as you have (then...)
27) Heb. 13:16	**Heb. 13:16**
16 ...for with such sacrifices God is well pleased	16 ...do not forget to do good ...and to share (for...)

Reflection Notes

LIFE TOPIC .4)

Symbolic Conditional Promises

Using word pictures

"She's as pretty as a picture."
"Life's a bowl of cherries."
"He's a chip off the old block."

Everyday, everywhere, people use words as pictures to express what they want to say. God uses them to reveal Himself to anyone who truly seeks to know Him in a personal way.

The fourth type of Conditional Promise recorded in this book was the first Symbolic Conditional Promise discovered in the Bible. A Symbolic Conditional Promise represents a picture, a shadow, or a type — which God uses to reveal Himself.

Symbolic Conditional Promises will be located at the end of each Life Topic chapter, and will be indicated by using a .4 immediately after the regular identifying number, as follows (i.e. 5.4 or 26.4).

Proverbs 1:8, 9

8 My son, hear the instruction of your father, and do not forsake the law of your mother;

9 for they will be a graceful ornament on your head, and chains about your neck.

34.4) Prov. 1:9	Prov. 1:8
	8 ...hear the instruction of your father ...do not forsake the law of your mother
9 ...for they (the instruction of your father) will be a graceful ornament on your head ...and (the law of your mother) (will be) chains about your neck	

GOD'S CONDITIONAL PROMISES — RESPONSIBILITIES OF THE DOER OF THE WORD

Symbolic Commentary:

If the young Doer of the Word will receive and follow the instruction of his parents with a positive and willing heart, his obedience will be turned into substantial blessings. He will become wise and others will take notice of his wisdom and find favor in him. God does not want the Doer of the Word to think of parental guidance and instruction as a burden, loaded down with a lot of negative don'ts.

There are two Conditional Promises God makes to us.

There are two responsibilities that we must do for God.

- Notice that the Commentary is an interpretation of the Symbolic Conditional Promise and provides an understanding in practical terms.

LIFE TOPIC 5

God, Man, and Society

Balanced relationship unity

The heartfelt cry for generations is "Why can't we all just get along?" The scrolls of history tell the agonizing story over and over of how our trying to get along has ended in failure. But God has never given up. Over the passage of time, man and society have played out their lives against the ever-present background of the affectionate heart of our loving Father — who unfolds — in His Conditional Promises — the amazing rewards available to us — when we do behave with godly (agape) love toward one another.

3 But know that the LORD has set apart for Himself him who is godly

GOD'S CONDITIONAL PROMISES	RESPONSIBILITIES OF THE DOER OF THE WORD
7) Ps. 4:3	Ps. 4:3
3 ...the LORD has set [many] apart for Himself him who...	3 ...(who) is godly

There is one Conditional Promise God makes to us.

There is one responsibility that we must do for God.

GOD'S CONDITIONAL PROMISES	RESPONSIBILITIES OF THE DOER OF THE WORD
7) Ps. 4:3	**Ps. 4:3**
3 ...the LORD has set [many] apart for Himself him who...	3 ...(who) is godly
14) Ps. 40:4	**Ps. 40:4**
4 Blessed is the man who...	4 ...(who) makes the LORD his trust ...(who) does not respect the proud ...(who does not) turn aside to lies
20) Ps. 86:5	**Ps. 86:5**
5 For You, LORD, are good... ...and ready to forgive... ...and abundant in mercy to all those who...	5 ...(who) call upon You
25) Ps. 106:3	**Ps. 106:3**
3 Blessed are those who... ...and he who...	3 ...(who) keep justice ...(who) does righteousness at all times
29) Ps. 118:26	**Ps. 118:26**
26 Blessed is he who...	26 ...(who) comes in the name of the LORD
33) Ps. 128:1	**Ps. 128:1**
1 Blessed [happy] is everyone who...	1 ...(who) fears the LORD ...who walks in His ways

God, Man, and Society LIFE TOPIC 5

GOD'S CONDITIONAL PROMISES	RESPONSIBILITIES OF THE DOER OF THE WORD
34) Ps. 146:5	**Ps. 146:5**
5 Happy [blessed] is he who...	5 ...(who) has the God of Jacob for his help ...whose hope is in the LORD his God
35) Ps. 146:8	**Ps.146:8**
8 The LORD loves...	8 ...(loves) the righteous
36) Ps. 147:11	**Ps. 147:11**
11 The LORD takes pleasure in those who... ...in those who...	11 ...(who) fear Him ...(who) hope in His mercy
38) Prov. 2:21	**Prov. 2:21**
21 ...will dwell in the land ...will remain in it [the land]	21 ...the upright (will...) ...the blameless (will...)
41) Prov. 3:33, 34, 35	**Prov. 3:33, 34, 35**
33 ... He blesses the home of... 34 ... (He) gives grace to... 35 ... shall inherit glory	33 ... (of) the just 34 ... (to) the humble 35 ... the wise (shall...)
43) Prov. 10:6, 7	**Prov. 10:6**
6 Blessings are on the head of... 7 The memory [as remembered by, spoken of, or held to by others] of the righteous is blessed	6 ... (of) the righteous

5 LIFE TOPIC — *God, Man, and Society*

GOD'S CONDITIONAL PROMISES	RESPONSIBILITIES OF THE DOER OF THE WORD
45) Prov. 11:18	**Prov. 11:18**
18 …he who… …will have a sure reward	18 …(who) sows righteousness (will have …)
48) Prov. 12:19	**Prov. 12:19**
19 …shall be established forever	19 The truthful lip (shall…)
49) Prov. 12:22	**Prov. 12:22**
22 …those who… …are His delight	22 …(who) deal truthfully (are…)
50) Prov. 13:13	**Prov. 13:13**
13 …he who… …will be rewarded	13 …(who) fears the commandment [the word of the LORD] (will…)
51) Prov. 13:18	**Prov. 13:18**
18 …he who… …will be honored	18 …(who) regards a rebuke (will…)
53) Prov. 15:8, 9	**Prov. 15:8, 9**
8 …the prayer of… …is His delight 9 He [God] loves him who…	8 …(of) the upright (is…) 9 …(who) follows righteousness
54) Prov. 15:21	**Prov. 15:21**
21 …a man of… …walks uprightly	21 …(of) understanding (walks…)

God, Man, and Society **LIFE TOPIC 5**

GOD'S CONDITIONAL PROMISES	RESPONSIBILITIES OF THE DOER OF THE WORD
57) Prov. 16:7	**Prov. 16:7**
7 ...He [God] makes even his enemies to be at peace with him	7 When a man's ways please the LORD (He...)
59) Prov. 18:16	**Prov. 18:16**
16 ...makes room for him ...and brings him before great men	16 A man's gift [food offering] (makes...)
61) Prov. 18:22	**Prov. 18:22**
22 He who... ...finds a good thing ...and obtains favor from the LORD	22 ...(who) finds a wife (finds...)
66) Prov. 22:11	**Prov. 22:11**
11 He who... ...the king [people in leadership positions] will be his friend	11 ...(who) loves purity of heart ...and has grace on his lips (the...)

5 LIFE TOPIC   *God, Man, and Society*

GOD'S CONDITIONAL PROMISES	RESPONSIBILITIES OF THE DOER OF THE WORD
69) Prov. 29:18	**Prov. 29:18**
18 ...happy [blessed] is he who...	18 ...(who) keeps the law [the Word of the LORD]
70) Prov. 30:5	**Prov. 30:5**
5 Every word of God is pure [tested, refined, found pure] He is a shield to those who...	5 ...(who) put their trust in Him
74) Isa. 49:23	**Isa. 49:23**
23 ...they shall not be ashamed who...	23 ...(who) wait for Me
78) Jer. 17:10	**Jer. 17:10**
10 I the LORD, search the heart... ...I (the LORD) test the mind, even to give every man...	10 ...(every man) according to his ways ...according to the fruit of his doings
81) Dan. 9:4	**Dan. 9:4**
4 O LORD, great and awesome God, who keeps His covenant ...and (keeps His) mercy with those who... ...and with those who...	4 ...(who) love Him ...(who) keep His commandments

GOD'S CONDITIONAL PROMISES	RESPONSIBILITIES OF THE DOER OF THE WORD
89) Matt. 5:7	Matt. 5:7
7 Blessed are... ...for they shall obtain mercy	7 ...(are) the merciful [compassionate, gentle, sympathetic] (for...)
90) Matt. 5:9	Matt. 5:9
9 Blessed are... ...for they shall be called sons of God	9 ...(are) the peacemakers (for...)
91) Matt. 5:16	Matt. 5:16
16 ...that they may see your good works ...and glorify your Father in heaven	16 Let your light so shine before men (that...)
93) Matt. 6:14	Matt. 6:14
14 ...if... ...your heavenly Father will also forgive you	14 ...(if) you forgive men their trespasses (your...)
95) Matt. 7:12	Matt. 7:12
12 ...whatever you want men to do to you...	12 ...(you) do also to them

GOD'S CONDITIONAL PROMISES	RESPONSIBILITIES OF THE DOER OF THE WORD
96) Mark 3:35	**Mark 3:35**
35 For whoever... ...is My brother and My sister and mother	35 ...(whoever) does the will of God (is...)
100) Luke 14:11	**Luke 14:11**
11 ...he who... ...will be exalted	11 ...he who humbles himself (will...)
104) John 9:31	**John 9:31**
31 ...if... ...He hears him	31 ...(if) anyone is a worshiper of God ...and does His will (He...)

Reflection Notes

LIFE TOPIC 6

Physical Health

Eating, drinking, exercise, and rest

Why wouldn't God want us to do an excellent job of maintaining our bodies? Our body is His temple. What we must be cautious of is focusing so much on our physical health that we become guilty of turning the care of our health into the worship of our bodies. Often, we make a greater effort to develop our bodies instead of developing our personal relationship with Jesus. Balance and moderation in all things is the healthiest way to live.

7 ... the children of men put their trust under the shadow of Your wings.

9 For with You is the fountain of life;

| | RESPONSIBILITIES OF |
GOD'S CONDITIONAL PROMISES	THE DOER OF THE WORD
7) Ps. 36:9	Ps. 36:7
	7 ...the children of men put their trust under the shadow of Your wings
9 For with You is the fountain of life	

There is one Conditional Promise God makes to us.

There is one responsibility that we must do for God.

6 LIFE TOPIC   *Physical Health*

GOD'S CONDITIONAL PROMISES	RESPONSIBILITIES OF THE DOER OF THE WORD
7) Ps. 36:9	**Ps. 36:7**
9 For with You is the fountain of life	7 ...the children of men put their trust under the shadow of Your wings
9) Ps. 91:16	**Ps. 91:2, 9**
16 With long life [length of days] I will satisfy him	2 I will say of the Lord, He is my refuge ...(He is)...my fortress ...(He is)...My God ...Him will I trust 9 Because you have made the Lord ...your dwelling place
15) Prov. 3:2	**Prov. 3:1**
2 ...for length of days... they will add to you ...(for) long life... they will add to you ...(for) peace...they will add to you	1 ...do not forget my law ...let your heart keep my commands

LIFE TOPIC 6

GOD'S CONDITIONAL PROMISES	RESPONSIBILITIES OF THE DOER OF THE WORD
16) Prov. 3:8	**Prov. 3:7**
	7 Do not be wise in your own eyes ...fear the Lord ...and depart from evil
8 It will be health to your flesh [body] ...(It will be) strength [refreshing drink] to your bones	
17) Prov. 4:10	**Prov. 4:10**
	10 Hear ... and receive my sayings (and...)
10 ... and the years of your life will be many	
19) Prov. 9:11, 12	**Prov. 9: 12**
11 ... by me (wisdom) your days will be multiplied ... years of life will be added to you 12 If...	12 (If) you are wise
20) Prov. 10:3	**Prov. 10:3**
3 The Lord will not allow ... ...to famish	3 ... (allow) the righteous soul (to...)

6 LIFE TOPIC — *Physical Health*

GOD'S CONDITIONAL PROMISES	RESPONSIBILITIES OF THE DOER OF THE WORD
22) Prov. 13:3	**Prov. 13:3**
3 He who... ...preserves his life	3 ...(who) guards his mouth (preserves...)
23) Prov. 15:4	**Prov. 15:4**
4 ...is a tree of life	4 A wholesome [healing] tongue (is...)
24) Prov. 15:13, 15	**Prov. 15:13, 15**
13 ...makes a cheerful countenance [face] 15 ...he who is of... ...has a continual feast	13 A merry heart (makes...) 15 ...(of) a merry heart (has...)
25) Prov. 16:24	**Prov. 16:24**
24 ...are like a honeycomb ...(are like) sweetness to the soul ...and (are like) health to the bones	24 Pleasant words (are...)

GOD'S CONDITIONAL PROMISES	RESPONSIBILITIES OF THE DOER OF THE WORD
26) Prov. 17:22	**Prov. 17:22**
22 ...does good, like medicine [makes medicine even better]	22 A merry heart (does...)
27) Prov. 18:14	**Prov. 18:14**
14 ...will sustain him in sickness	14 The spirit of a man (will...)
29) Prov. 28:14	**Prov. 28:14**
14 Happy is the man who...	14 ...(who) is always reverent
30) Eccl. 5:12	**Eccl. 5:12**
12 The sleep of... ...is sweet	12 ...(of) a laboring man (is...)
32) Eccl. 8:1	**Eccl. 8:1**
1 ...makes his face shine ...and the sternness of his face is changed	1 A man's wisdom (makes...)

6 LIFE TOPIC   *Physical Health*

GOD'S CONDITIONAL PROMISES	RESPONSIBILITIES OF THE DOER OF THE WORD
35) Matt. 6:22	Matt. 6:22
22 The lamp of the body is the eye. If therefore... ...your whole body will be full of light	22 ...(If therefore) your eye is good (your...)
39) Rom. 8:6	Rom. 8:6
6 ...is life ...and (is) peace	6 ...to be spiritually minded (is...)
43) 1 Tim. 4:4	1 Tim. 4:4
4 ...every creature of God is good and... ...if...	4 ...(and) nothing is to be refused ...(if) it is received with thanksgiving
44) 1 Tim. 4:8	1 Tim. 4:8
8 ...profits a little, but... ...is profitable for all things	8 ...bodily exercise (profits...) ...(but) godliness (is...)
45) Titus 1:15	Titus 1:15
15 ...all things are pure	15 To the pure (all...)
46) 1 Pet. 5:14	1 Pet. 5:14
14 Peace to you all who...	14 Greet one another with a kiss of love ...(who) are in Christ Jesus

Reflection Notes

LIFE TOPIC 7

Leadership and Authority

Personal, business, or ministry work

Jesus showed us that a true leader serves others, and does not treat others as though he must be served himself. A true leader plans out the work to be done, applies diligence and discipline, upholds a model that is worth following, and gives God all the glory for the results.

Psalm 115:13

13 He will bless those who fear the
   Lord, both small and great.

<table>
<tr><td></td><td style="text-align:center">GOD'S CONDITIONAL PROMISES</td><td style="text-align:center">RESPONSIBILITIES OF
THE DOER OF THE WORD</td></tr>
</table>

6) Ps. 115:13	Ps. 115:13
13 He will bless those who… …both [that are] great [in position, size or number]	13 …(who) fear the Lord (both…)

There are two Conditional Promises God makes to us.
There is one responsibility that we must do for God.

7 LIFE TOPIC *Leadership and Authority*

GOD'S CONDITIONAL PROMISES	RESPONSIBILITIES OF THE DOER OF THE WORD
6) Ps. 115:13	Ps. 115:13
13 He will bless those who... ...both [that are] great [in position, size or number]	13 ...(who) fear the Lord (both...)
10) Ps. 127:1	Ps. 127:1
1 ...they labor in vain who build it	1 Unless the Lord build the house [the affairs of your life] (they...)
12) Ps. 147:6	Ps. 147:6
6 The Lord lifts up...	6 ...(up) the humble
15) Prov. 11:3	Prov. 11:3
3 The integrity of... ... will guide them	3 ... (of) the upright (will...)
16) Prov. 12:24	Prov. 12:24
24 The hand of... ...will rule	24 ...(of) the diligent (will...)
18) Prov. 15:19	Prov. 15:19
19 ...the way of ...is a highway	19 ...(of) the upright (is...)

Leadership and Authority LIFE TOPIC 7

GOD'S CONDITIONAL PROMISES	RESPONSIBILITIES OF THE DOER OF THE WORD
19) Prov. 16:3	Prov. 16:3
3 ...and your thoughts will be established	3 Commit [wholly surrender with trust] your works to the Lord (and...)
21) Prov. 28:20	Prov. 28:20
20 ...will abound with blessings	20 A faithful man (will...)
23) Prov. 29:23	Prov. 29:23
23 ...will retain honor	23 ...the humble in spirit (will...)
24) Eccl. 7:8	Eccl. 7:8
8 ...is better than the proud spirit	8 ...the patient in spirit (is...)
28) Luke 6:40	Luke 6:40
40 A disciple is not above his teacher, but everyone who... ...will be like his teacher	40 ...(who) is perfectly trained (will...)
46) James 3:1	James 3:1
1 ...that we shall receive a stricter judgment	1 ...let not many of you become teachers ...knowing (that...)

LIFE 8
TOPIC

Stewardship

Managing money, material
things, and time

When we come to understand and truly embrace the
fact that God owns everything, it clears and calms our
minds to understand that God desires us to be faithful
managers, not co-owners of anything. When God can
entrust the wealth of this world into our hands, there
will be no shame in knowing — that He often allows
us to enjoy it also.

Psalm 1:1, 2, 3

1 Blessed is the man who walks not in the counsel of the ungodly, nor stands in the path of sinners, nor sits in the seat of the scornful;

2 but his delight is in the law of the LORD, And in His law he meditates day and night.

3 He shall be like a tree Planted by the rivers of water, That brings forth its fruit in its season, Whose leaf also shall not wither; And whatever he does shall prosper.

GOD'S CONDITIONAL PROMISES		RESPONSIBILITIES OF THE DOER OF THE WORD	
5) Ps. 1:1, 3		**Ps. 1:1, 2**	
1	Blessed is the man who…	1	…(who) walks not in the counsel of the ungodly [wicked] …nor stands in the path of sinners …nor sits in the seat of the scornful
		2	…but his delight is in the law of the Lord …and in His law he meditates [ponders by thinking to himself] day and night
3	…whatever he does shall prosper		

There are two Conditional Promises God makes to us.

There are five responsibilities that we must do for God.

GOD'S CONDITIONAL PROMISES	RESPONSIBILITIES OF THE DOER OF THE WORD
5) Ps. 1:1, 3	**Ps. 1:1, 2**
1 Blessed is the man who...	1 ...(who) walks not in the counsel of the ungodly [wicked] ...nor stands in the path of sinners ...nor sits in the seat of the scornful 2 ...but his delight is in the law of the Lord ...and in His law he meditates [ponders by thinking to himself] day and night
3 ...whatever he does shall prosper	
9) Ps. 34:9, 10	**Ps. 34:9, 10**
9 There is no want [lack] to those who... 10 ...but those who... ... shall not lack any good thing	9 ...(who) fear the Lord 10 ...(who) seek the Lord (shall...)
18) Ps. 128:2	**Ps. 128:2**
	2 When you eat the labor [fruit] of your hands (you...)
2 ...you shall be happy ...and it shall be well with you	

GOD'S CONDITIONAL PROMISES	RESPONSIBILITIES OF THE DOER OF THE WORD
20) Prov. 10:4, 5	**Prov. 10:4, 5**
4 … the hand of… …makes rich 5 He who… … is a wise son	4 … (of) the diligent (makes…) 5 … (who) gathers in the summer (is…)
21) Prov. 11:15	**Prov. 11:15**
15 …one who… …is secure	15 … (who) hates being surety [pledging guarantee] (is…)
22) Prov. 12:11, 12	**Prov. 12:11, 12**
11 He who… …will be satisfied with bread 12 …the root of… …yields fruit	11 …(who) tills [works for, cultivates] his land (will…) 12 …(of) the righteous (yields…)
23) Prov. 12:14	**Prov. 12:14**
14 A man will be satisfied with good by… …the recompense of… …will be rendered to him	14 …(by) the fruit of his mouth …(of) a man's hands (will…)
24) Prov. 13:2	**Prov. 13:2**
2 A man shall eat well by…	2 …(by) the fruit of his mouth

8 LIFE TOPIC — *Stewardship*

GOD'S CONDITIONAL PROMISES	RESPONSIBILITIES OF THE DOER OF THE WORD
25) Prov. 13:4	**Prov. 13:4**
4 ...the soul of... ...shall be made rich	4 ...(of) the diligent (shall...)
26) Prov. 13:11	**Prov. 13:11**
11 ...he who... ...will increase	11 ...(who) gathers by labor (will...)
27) Prov. 14:11	**Prov. 14:11**
11 ...the tent of... ...will flourish	11 ...(of) the upright (will...)
28) Prov. 14:23	**Prov. 14:23**
23 ...there is profit	23 In all labor (there...)
29) Prov. 15:6	**Prov. 15:6**
6 In the house of ...there is much treasure	6 ...(of) the righteous (there...)

GOD'S CONDITIONAL PROMISES	RESPONSIBILITIES OF THE DOER OF THE WORD
30) Prov. 18:20	Prov. 18:20
20 A man's stomach shall be satisfied from... ...he shall be filled	20 ...(from) the fruit of his mouth ...from the produce of his lips (he...)
31) Prov. 20:13	Prov. 20:13
13 ...and you will be satisfied with bread	13 ...open your eyes (and...)
32) Prov. 21:5	Prov. 21:5
5 The plans of... ...lead surely to plenty	5 ...(of) the diligent (lead...)
33) Prov. 22:4	Prov. 22:4
4 ...(are) riches	4 By humility ...and the fear of the Lord (are...)
35) Prov. 28:25	Prov. 28:25
25 ..he who... ...will be prospered	25 ...(who) trusts in the Lord (will...)

8 LIFE TOPIC   *Stewardship*

GOD'S CONDITIONAL PROMISES	RESPONSIBILITIES OF THE DOER OF THE WORD
36) Isa. 1:19	**Isa. 1:19**
19 If... ...you shall eat the good of the land	19 (If) you are willing ...and (you are) obedient (you...)
42) Luke 16:10	**Luke 16:10**
10 He who... ...is faithful also in much	10 ...(who) is faithful in what is least (is...)

Reflection Notes

LIFE 9
TOPIC

Backsliding

Returning to God from living in sin

At first, sin usually seems fun and somewhat harmless. Then, if we decide we want to be free of it, we may find its grip too strong to break. After a while, it's easier to remain lost in its ways than to believe God can and will accept us back into His fellowship — much less believe that He will restore us into a place of usefulness and prosperity.

Psalm 51:3, 17

3 For I acknowledge my transgressions ...

17 the sacrifices of God are a broken spirit, a broken and a contrite heart — these, O God, You will not despise

GOD'S CONDITIONAL PROMISES	RESPONSIBILITIES OF THE DOER OF THE WORD
3) Ps. 51:17	Ps. 51:3, 17
	3 For I acknowledge my transgressions 17 ...a broken spirit ...a broken...heart ...a contrite... heart (these...)
17 ...these, O God, You will not despise	

There is one Conditional Promise God makes to us.

There are four responsibilities that we must do for God.

9 LIFE TOPIC   *Backsliding*

GOD'S CONDITIONAL PROMISES	RESPONSIBILITIES OF THE DOER OF THE WORD
3) Ps. 51:17	Ps. 51:3, 17
17 ...these, O God, You will not despise	3 For I acknowledge my transgressions 17 ...a broken spirit ...a broken...heart ...a contrite... heart (these...)
5) Prov. 3:12	Prov. 3:11
12 ... for whom the Lord loves He corrects, just as a father (corrects) the son in whom he delights	11 ... do not despise the chastening of the Lord ... nor (do not) detest His correction
6) Prov. 16:6	Prov. 16:6
6 ...atonement is provided for iniquity [sins] and... ...one departs from evil	6 In mercy and truth (atonement...) ...(and) by the fear [utmost reverence] of the Lord (one...)

Backsliding   LIFE TOPIC **9**

GOD'S CONDITIONAL PROMISES	RESPONSIBILITIES OF THE DOER OF THE WORD
11) Isa. 55:7	Isa. 55:6, 7
7 ...and He will have mercy on him ...for He will abundantly pardon	6 Seek the Lord while He may be found ...call upon Him while He is near 7 Let the wicked [man of iniquity] forsake his way ...and (Let) the unrighteous man (forsake) his thoughts ...return to the Lord (and...)
21) Zech. 1:3	Zech. 1:3, 4
3 ...and I will return to you, says the Lord of hosts	3 ...return to Me (and...) 4 Do not be like your fathers, to whom the former prophets preached, saying, Thus says the Lord of hosts: Turn now from your evil ways and your evil deeds. But they did not hear nor heed Me
22) Mal. 3:6, 7	Mal. 3:7
6 For I am the Lord, I do not change... 7 ...and I will return to you	7 Return to Me (and...)

9 LIFE TOPIC

Backsliding

GOD'S CONDITIONAL PROMISES	RESPONSIBILITIES OF THE DOER OF THE WORD
23) Luke 15:7, 10	**Luke 15:7, 10**
7 …there will be more joy in heaven over one sinner who… …than over ninety-nine just persons who need no repentance 10 …there is joy in the presence of the angels of God over one sinner who…	7 …(who) repents (than…) 10 …(who) repents
24) Heb. 12:6, 7, 9, 11	**Heb. 12:5, 7, 9, 11**
    6 …for whom the Lord loves He chastens …and scourges every son whom He receives 7 If… …God deals with you as with sons 9 …and live 11 …afterward it yields the peaceable fruit of righteousness to those who…	5 …do not despise the chastening of the Lord …Nor be discouraged when you are rebuked by Him 7 (If) you endure chastening 9 …be in subjection to the Father of spirits (and…) 11 …(who) have been trained by it

GOD'S CONDITIONAL PROMISES	RESPONSIBILITIES OF THE DOER OF THE WORD
25) James 5:19, 20	James 5:20
19 Brethren, if anyone among you wanders from the truth, and someone turns him back 20 let him know that he who… …will save a soul from death and cover a multitude of sins	20 …(who) turns a sinner from the error of his way (will…)

LIFE TOPIC 10

Older Generation

Mature, seasoned adulthood

While the word "great" can be a subjective term, here God is distinguishing the vast difference between being among those who are young, in contrast to those who are elderly and experienced on this journey of life.

God's Conditional Promises to the elderly are a sure commitment that He will keep them and always provide for all they need.

13 He will bless those who fear the
LORD, ... both [those who are]
great [elderly in age]

GOD'S CONDITIONAL PROMISES	RESPONSIBILITIES OF THE DOER OF THE WORD
1) Ps. 115:13	Ps. 115:13
13 He will bless those who... ...both [those who are] great [elderly in age]	13 ...(who) fear the Lord (both...)

There are two Conditional Promise God makes to us.

There is one responsibility that we must do for God.

10 LIFE TOPIC — *Older Generation*

| | RESPONSIBILITIES OF |
| GOD'S CONDITIONAL PROMISES | THE DOER OF THE WORD |

1) Ps. 115:13	Ps. 115:13
13 He will bless those who... ...both [those who are] great [elderly in age]	13 ...(who) fear the Lord (both...)
2) Prov. 12:28	Prov. 12:28
28 In the way of... ...is life ...in its pathway there is no death	28 ...(of) righteousness (is...)
3) Prov. 16:31	Prov. 16:31
31 The silver-haired head is a crown of glory, if it is found in the way of...	31 ...(of) righteousness
4) Prov. 20:29	Prov. 20:29
29 The splendor of old men is...	29 ...(is) their gray head
5) Prov. 22:4	Prov. 22:4
    4 ...(are) life	4 by humility ...and the fear of the Lord (are...)

GOD'S CONDITIONAL PROMISES	RESPONSIBILITIES OF THE DOER OF THE WORD
6) Prov. 28:16	**Prov. 28:16**
16 ...he who... ...will prolong his days	16 ...(who) hates covetousness (will...)
7) Eccl. 7:12	**Eccl. 7:12**
12 ...the excellence [advantage or profit] of knowledge is that wisdom gives life to those who...	12 ...(who) have it [knowledge]
8) Isa. 46:4	**Isa. 46:3**
4 Even to your old age, I am He (I will carry you) ...and even to gray hairs I will carry you ...I have made, and I will bear ...even I will carry (you) ...and (I) will deliver you	3 Listen [diligently and intelligently obedient] to Me
9) Eph. 6:1, 3	**Eph. 6:2**
1 ...for this is right 3 ...that it may be well with you ...and you may live long on the earth	2 Honor your father ...and (honor your) mother

LIFE TOPIC 11

Confrontation

Relationship or circumstantial barriers

Confrontation is part of life. It is a major part of what God allows to happen to shape our character, teach us, and mature us. To receive the benefits God desires for us, we are required to stay mindful that we are not abandoned by God during such times. When we have confidence and courage in the face of confrontation because of Him, we will not feel fear, but will feel secure in Him.

2 Chronicles 16:9

9 For the eyes of the LORD run to and fro throughout the whole earth, to show Himself strong on behalf of those whose heart is loyal to Him.

GOD'S CONDITIONAL PROMISES	RESPONSIBILITIES OF THE DOER OF THE WORD
3) 2 Chron. 16:9	2 Chron. 16:9
9 …the eyes of the Lord run to and fro throughout the whole earth, to show Himself strong on behalf of those…	9 …(those) whose heart is loyal to Him

There is one Conditional Promise God makes to us.
There is one responsibility that we must do for God.

GOD'S CONDITIONAL PROMISES	RESPONSIBILITIES OF THE DOER OF THE WORD
3) 2 Chron. 16:9	2 Chron. 16:9
9 ...the eyes of the Lord run to and fro throughout the whole earth, to show Himself strong on behalf of those...	9 ...(those) whose heart is loyal to Him
11) Ps. 20:6	Ps. 20:7, 8
6 ...the Lord saves His anointed ...He will answer him from His holy heaven with this saving strength of His right hand	7 ...remember the name of the Lord our God 8 ...we have risen and stand upright
15) Ps. 46:1, 7	Ps. 46:2
1 God is our refuge ...(God is our) strength ...a very present [abundantly available] help in trouble 7 The Lord of hosts is with us ...the God of Jacob is our refuge	2 (Therefore) we will not fear

Confrontation LIFE TOPIC 11

GOD'S CONDITIONAL PROMISES	RESPONSIBILITIES OF THE DOER OF THE WORD
26) Prov. 2:7, 8	Prov. 2:7
7 ...He is a shield to those who... 8 ...He guards the paths of justice ...and (He) preserves the way of his saints	7 ...(who) walk uprightly
27) Prov. 3:26	Prov. 3:25
26 ...the Lord will be your confidence ...(the Lord will) keep your foot from being caught	25 Do not be afraid of sudden terror ...(Do not be afraid of) trouble from the wicked when it comes
28) Prov. 12:13	Prov. 12:13
13 ...will come through trouble	13 ...the righteous (will...)
29) Prov. 21:23	Prov. 21:23
23 Whoever... ...keeps his soul from troubles	23 ...(Whoever) guards his mouth ...(whoever guards his) tongue (keeps...)

11 LIFE TOPIC   *Confrontation*

GOD'S CONDITIONAL PROMISES	RESPONSIBILITIES OF THE DOER OF THE WORD
30) Prov. 29:25	**Prov. 29:25**
25 …whoever… …shall be safe [secure, set on high]	25 …(whoever) trusts in the Lord (shall…)
34) Nah. 1:7	**Nah. 1:7**
7 …The Lord is good …(The Lord is) a stronghold in the day of trouble …and He knows those who…	 7 …(who) trust in Him
35) Zeph. 3:19	**Zeph. 3:14, 16**
       19 …I will deal with all who afflict you	14 Sing …Shout …Be glad …and rejoice with all your heart 16 Do not fear …let not your hands be weak
36) Mark 9:23	**Mark 9:23**
23 If… …all things are possible to him who believes	23 …(If) you can believe (all…)

GOD'S CONDITIONAL PROMISES	RESPONSIBILITIES OF THE DOER OF THE WORD
38) Rom. 8:28	Rom. 8:28
28 And we know that all things work together for good to those who… …to those who… …according to His purpose	28 …(who) love God …(who) are the called (according…)
42) 1 John 4:18	1 John 4:18
18 There is no fear in love; but… …casts out fear	18 …(but) perfect love (casts…)
43) Rev. 21:7	Rev. 21:7
7 He who… …shall inherit all things …and I will be his God …and he shall be My son	7 …(who) overcomes (shall…)

LIFE TOPIC 12

Anxiety, depression, and oppression

God's provision for overcoming

Our hope is built on nothing less than Jesus Christ and His righteousness. When life comes at you hard, it is the full armor of God and His Conditional Promises that make your battles winnable. Knowing that He has promised to heal the brokenhearted should make us want to thank Him when adversity strikes and praise Him for as long as it remains — which is exactly what He asks us to do.

Psalm 4:1

1 Hear me when I call, O God of my righteousness! You have relieved me in my distress;

GOD'S CONDITIONAL PROMISES	RESPONSIBILITIES OF THE DOER OF THE WORD
1) Ps. 4:1	Ps. 4:1
	1 …when I call, O God of my righteousness (You…)
1 …You have relieved me in my distress	

There is one Conditional Promise God makes to us.

There is one responsibility that we must do for God.

12 LIFE TOPIC — *Anxiety, depression, and oppression*

GOD'S CONDITIONAL PROMISES	RESPONSIBILITIES OF THE DOER OF THE WORD
1) Ps. 4:1	Ps. 4:1
	1 ...when I call, O God of my righteousness (You...)
1 ...You have relieved me in my distress	
8) Ps. 37:4, 5	Ps. 37:3, 4, 5
	3 Trust in the Lord ...do good ...dwell in the land ...feed on His faithfulness
	4 Delight yourself also in the Lord (and...)
4 ...and He shall give you the desires of your heart	
	5 Commit your way to the Lord ...trust also in Him (and...)
5 ...and He shall bring it to pass	
10) Ps. 50:15	Ps. 50:15
	15 Call upon Me (in...)
15 ...in the day of trouble; I will deliver you ...and You shall glorify Me	
16) Ps. 119:114	Ps. 119:114, 115
114 You are my hiding place ...(You are my) shield...	
	114 ...(shield) I hope in Your word
	115 ...I will keep the commandments of my God

Anxiety, depression, and oppression

LIFE TOPIC 12

GOD'S CONDITIONAL PROMISES	RESPONSIBILITIES OF THE DOER OF THE WORD
19) Ps. 144:15	**Ps. 144:9, 15**
15 Happy are the people who… …happy are the people whose…	9 I will sing a new song to You, O God …I will sing praises to You 15 …(who) are in such a state …(whose) God is the Lord
20) Ps. 145:18	**Ps. 145:18**
18 The Lord is near to all who… …to all who…	18 …(who) call upon Him …(who) call upon Him in truth
23) Ps. 147:3	**Ps. 147:1**
3 He heals the brokenhearted …and (He) binds up their wounds [sorrows]	1 Praise the Lord
25) Prov. 12:6	**Prov. 12:6**
6 …the mouth of… …will deliver them	6 …(of) the upright (will…)
26) Prov. 12:20, 21	**Prov. 12:20, 21**
20 …have joy 21 No grave trouble [harm] will overtake…	20 …counselors of peace (have…) 21 …(overtake) the righteous

12 **LIFE** TOPIC *Anxiety, depression, and oppression*

GOD'S CONDITIONAL PROMISES	RESPONSIBILITIES OF THE DOER OF THE WORD
27) Prov. 13:21	Prov. 13:21
21 ...good shall be repaid	21 ...to the righteous (good...)
28) Prov. 18:10	Prov. 18:10
10 The name of the Lord is a strong tower... ...and are safe [secure, set on high]	10 ...(tower) the righteous run in it (and...)
29) Isa. 26:3, 4	Isa. 26:3, 4
3 You will keep him in perfect peace, whose... 4 ...for in YAH, the Lord, is everlasting [Rock of Ages] strength	3 ...(whose) mind is stayed on You ...because he trusts in you 4 Trust in the Lord forever (for...)
30) Isa. 40:31	Isa. 40:31
31 ...those who... ...shall renew their strength ...they shall mount up with wings like eagles ...they shall run and not be weary ...they shall walk and not faint	31 ...(who) wait on the Lord (shall...)

Anxiety, depression, and oppression

LIFE TOPIC 12

GOD'S CONDITIONAL PROMISES	RESPONSIBILITIES OF THE DOER OF THE WORD
31) Isa. 41:10	**Isa. 41:10**
10 ...for I am with you ...for I am your God ...I will strengthen you ...I will uphold you with My righteous right hand	10 ...fear not (for...) ...be not dismayed (for...)
33) Isa. 57:1, 2	**Isa. 57:1**
1 ...is taken away from [the face of] evil 2 ...he shall enter into peace ...they shall rest in their beds	1 ...the righteous (is...)
39) Rom. 8:28	**Rom. 8:28**
28 And we know that all things work together for good to those who... ...to those who... ...according to His purpose	28 ...(who) love God ...(who) are the called (according...)

12 LIFE TOPIC *Anxiety, depression, and oppression*

GOD'S CONDITIONAL PROMISES	RESPONSIBILITIES OF THE DOER OF THE WORD
44) Phil. 4:9	**Phil. 4:8, 9**
	8 ...whatever things are true ...whatever things are noble ...whatever things are just ...whatever things are pure ...whatever things are lovely ...whatever things are of good report ...if there is any virtue ...and if there is anything praiseworthy ...meditate on these things 9 The things which you learned ...and (the things which you) received ...and (the things which you) heard ...and (the things which you) saw in me, these do (and...)
9 ...and the God of peace will be with you	
50) 1 Pet. 5:7	**1 Pet. 5:7**
	7 ...casting all your care upon Him (for...)
7 ...for [because] He cares for you	

GOD'S CONDITIONAL PROMISES	RESPONSIBILITIES OF THE DOER OF THE WORD
51) 1 Pet. 5:10	1 Pet. 5:10
10 ...may the God of all grace ...who called us to His eternal glory by Christ Jesus, after... ...perfect ...establish ...strengthen ...and settle you	10 ...(after) you have suffered a while (perfect...)
52) 1 John 4:18	1 John 4:18
18 There is no fear in love; but... ...casts out fear	18 ...(but) perfect love (casts...)

LIFE TOPIC 13

The Poor

Homeless, abandoned, widowed, and parentless

Jesus' words, "the kingdom of God is at hand" not only referred to Himself as He walked the earth, but also refers to us, who come to Him and hear His sayings and do them (Luke 6:46-49). The poor receive the blessings of the Conditional Promises of God through Christians and non-Christians — through *all* who give from their financial and material wealth.

Psalm 9:18

18 For the needy shall not always be
   forgotten; the expectation of the
   poor shall not perish forever.

GOD'S CONDITIONAL PROMISES	RESPONSIBILITIES OF THE DOER OF THE WORD
1) Ps. 9:18	Ps. 9:18
18 ...shall not perish forever	18 the expectation [hoping or looking forward] of the poor (shall...)

There is one Conditional Promise God makes to us.

There is one responsibility that we must do for God.

13 LIFE TOPIC — *The Poor*

GOD'S CONDITIONAL PROMISES	RESPONSIBILITIES OF THE DOER OF THE WORD
1) Ps. 9:18	Ps. 9:18
	18 the expectation [hoping or looking forward] of the poor (shall...)
18 ...shall not perish forever	
2) Ps. 10:14, 17, 18	Ps. 10:14, 17
14 ...You are the helper of the fatherless	14 The helpless commits [leaves, entrusts] himself to You [the Lord God]
17 Lord, You have heard the desire of... ...You will prepare their [the humble] heart ...You will cause Your ear to hear	17 ...(of) the humble
18 ...to do justice to [vindicate] the fatherless	
3) Ps. 12:5; 14:6	Ps. 13:5, 6
5 For the oppression of the poor...I will arise, says the Lord ...for the sighing of the needy...(I will arise, says the Lord) ...I will set him in safety for which he yearns	
	5 ...I have trusted in Your mercy ...my heart shall rejoice in Your salvation
	6 I will sing to the Lord
6 ...the Lord is his refuge	

The Poor   LIFE TOPIC **13**

GOD'S CONDITIONAL PROMISES	RESPONSIBILITIES OF THE DOER OF THE WORD
6) Ps. 102:17	Ps. 102:17
17 He shall regard the prayer of... ...and (He) shall not despise their prayer	17 ...(of) the destitute (and...)
14) Prov. 13:6	Prov. 13:6
6 Righteousness guards him whose...	6 ...(whose) way is blameless
15) Prov. 15:25	Prov. 15:25
25 ...He will establish the boundary of...	25 ...(of) the widow
16) Rom. 8:28	Rom. 8:28
28 And we know that all things work together for good to those who... ...to those who ...according to His purpose	28 ...(who) love God ...(who) are the called (according...)

LIFE TOPIC 14

Angels

Our authority and their assistance

Since this book is the *Condensed Edition* of *The Conditional Promises of God*, not all of the Conditional Promises of God regarding His blessings are printed in their expanded form, as they are in the *Unabridged Edition*. Life Topics 1 and 14 are omitted from the Condensed Edition, and are found in their entirety in the Unabridged Edition.

The Unabridged Edition is available from www.TheConditionalPromisesOfGod.org.

LIFE TOPIC 15

Persecution

Finding hope, strength, and courage

Society has placed such a high regard on one's personal rights, that the idea of having to suffer persecution is almost nonexistent. Fighting back or getting even has become the norm. God says we will suffer persecution because of our belief in Him, and that through His Conditional Promises, we can see it as a doorway to opportunity and blessing — not to anguish and despair.

Psalm 115:11

11 You who fear the LORD, trust in the LORD; He is their help and their shield.

GOD'S CONDITIONAL PROMISES	RESPONSIBILITIES OF THE DOER OF THE WORD
6) Ps. 115:11	Ps. 115:11
	11 You who fear the Lord, …(you who) trust in the Lord (He…)
11 …He is their help …(He is) their shield	

There are two Conditional Promises God makes to us.

There are two responsibilities that we must do for God.

15 LIFE TOPIC   *Persecution*

GOD'S CONDITIONAL PROMISES	RESPONSIBILITIES OF THE DOER OF THE WORD
6) Ps. 115:11	**Ps. 115:11**
11 …He is their help …(He is) their shield	11 You who fear the Lord, …(you who) trust in the Lord (He…)
8) Ps. 119:86	**Ps. 119:81, 83**
86 All Your commandments are faithful	81 …I hope in Your word 83 …I do not forget Your statutes
11) Prov. 28:10	**Prov. 28:10**
10 …will inherit good	10 …the blameless (will…)
12) Prov. 28:18	**Prov. 28:18**
18 Whoever… …will be saved [delivered]	18 …(whoever) walks blamelessly (will…)
13) Prov. 28:26	**Prov. 28:26**
26 …whoever… …will be delivered	26 …(whoever) walks wisely (will…)

Persecution

LIFE TOPIC 15

GOD'S CONDITIONAL PROMISES	RESPONSIBILITIES OF THE DOER OF THE WORD
14) Eccl. 8:12	Eccl. 8:12
12 Though a sinner does evil a hundred times, and his days are prolonged, yet I surely know that it will be well with those who...	12 ...(who) fear God ...(who) fear before Him
23) Matt. 10:39	Matt. 10:39
39 ...he who... ...will find it	39 ...(who) loses his life for My sake (will...)
24) Matt. 16:25	Matt. 16:25
25 ...whoever... ...will find it	25 ...(whoever) loses his life for My sake (will...)
26) Luke 6:22, 23	Luke 6:23
22 Blessed are you when men hate you... ...and when they exclude you ...and revile you ...and cast out your name as evil, for the Son of Man's sake 23 ...For indeed your reward is great in heaven, for in like manner their fathers did to the prophets	23 Rejoice in that day ...and leap for joy (For...)

15 LIFE TOPIC   *Persecution*

GOD'S CONDITIONAL PROMISES	RESPONSIBILITIES OF THE DOER OF THE WORD
31) John 16:33	**John 16:33**
33 These things I have spoken to you, that in Me you may have peace In the world you will have tribulation; but... ...I have overcome the world	33 ...(but) be of good cheer (I...)
33) Rom. 8:28	**Rom. 8:28**
28 And we know that all things work together for good to those who... ...to those who ...according to His purpose	28 ...(who) love God ...(who) are the called (according...)
34) Rom. 8:38, 39	**Rom. 8:38**
38 ...nor things present ...nor things to come... 39 ...shall be able to separate us from the love of God which is in Christ Jesus our Lord	38 ...I am persuaded

Persecution

GOD'S CONDITIONAL PROMISES	RESPONSIBILITIES OF THE DOER OF THE WORD
36) 2 Cor. 1:3, 4, 7	**2 Cor. 1:4, 7**
3 Blessed be the God and Father of our Lord Jesus Christ the Father of mercies ...and God of all comfort 4 ...who comforts us in all our tribulation ...that we may be able to comfort those who are in any trouble...	
	4 ...(trouble) with the comfort with which we ourselves are comforted by God
7 ...so also you will partake of the consolation [comfort]	7 ...as you are partakers of the sufferings (so...)
39) 2 Tim. 3:12	**2 Tim. 3:12**
12 Yes, and all who... ...will suffer persecution	12...(who) desire to live godly in Christ Jesus (will...)

15 LIFE TOPIC   *Persecution*

GOD'S CONDITIONAL PROMISES	RESPONSIBILITIES OF THE DOER OF THE WORD
42) James 1:3, 4	James 1:2, 3, 4
	2 ...count it all joy when you fall into various trials 3 ...knowing (that...)
3 ...that the testing of your faith produces patience [endurance or perseverance]	
	4 ...let patience have its perfect work (that...)
4 ...that you may be perfect [mature] ...and complete ...lacking nothing	

GOD'S CONDITIONAL PROMISES	RESPONSIBILITIES OF THE DOER OF THE WORD
51.4) Isa. 54:15	Isa. 54:1, 2, 4
	1 Sing …break forth into singing …cry aloud 2 Enlarge the place of your tent …stretch out the curtains of your dwellings …do not spare; lengthen your cords …strengthen your stakes 4 Do not fear
15 Whoever assembles against you shall fall for your sake	

Symbolic Commentary
Worship is the one true response that God desires. He is worthy of all praise, worship, and thanksgiving (Ps. 92:1-2). When God tells the doer of the Word to stretch out the curtains of his dwelling, lengthen his cords, and strengthen his stakes; he is directed to adjust his attitude, to rise above his depression and choose not to linger on hurt feelings. He should cast his cares on the Lord, because He cares for him (1 Pet. 5:7) and sing out loud to God the Father.

LIFE TOPIC 16

Death

Never needing to fear it at any age

Each person, at some time in his life, will lose his mortal body. Seeing your death from God's perspective should change everything about how you live. By living today like it will be your last on earth, you will discover if you have God's perspective about dying. Enjoy every age — and rejoice in every stage of life, in oneness with Him. Then when it is time to enjoy the next stage of your "new life," you will be ready. "'Fear not, for I am with you,' … says the Lord" (Isaiah 41:10, 14, NKJV).

18 The Lᴏʀᴅ knows the days of
the upright, and their inheritance
shall be forever.

GOD'S CONDITIONAL PROMISES	RESPONSIBILITIES OF THE DOER OF THE WORD
1) Ps. 37:18	Ps. 37:18
18 The Lord knows the days of... ...and their inheritance shall be forever	18 ...(of) the upright (and...)

There are two Conditional Promises God makes to us.

There is one responsibility that we must do for God.

16 LIFE TOPIC — *Death*

GOD'S CONDITIONAL PROMISES	RESPONSIBILITIES OF THE DOER OF THE WORD
1) Ps. 37:18	Ps. 37:18
18 The Lord knows the days of... ...and their inheritance shall be forever	18 ...(of) the upright (and...)
2) Ps. 49:15	Ps. 49:5
15 ...God will redeem my soul from the power of the grave ...for He shall receive me	5 Why should I fear in the days of evil
3) Ps. 116:15	Ps. 116:15
15 Precious in the sight of the Lord is...	15 ...(is) the death of His saints
4) Ps. 118:20	Ps. 118:20
20 This is the gate of the Lord, through which... ...shall enter	20 ...(which) the righteous (shall...)

GOD'S CONDITIONAL PROMISES	RESPONSIBILITIES OF THE DOER OF THE WORD
6) John 8:51	**John 8:51**
51 Most assuredly, I say to you, if anyone… …he shall never see death	51 …(if) anyone keeps My word (he…)
7) Rom. 8:38, 39	**Rom. 8:38**
38 …neither death …nor life… 39 …shall be able to separate us from the love of God which is in Christ Jesus our Lord	38 …I am persuaded
15) Rev. 14:13	**Rev. 14:13**
13 …Blessed are the dead who… …Yes, says the Spirit, that they may rest from their labors …and (Yes, says the Spirit, that) their works follow them	13 …(who) die in the Lord from now on (Yes…)

LIFE TOPIC 17

Wisdom

Instruction and direction
for making decisions

God made us to have free-will choice — and life is
about making choices. By learning — we gain knowledge. In living — we gain experience. With matu-
rity — comes understanding. Therefore, all together,
knowledge is what you know — and wisdom is what
you do with what you know — and through the pass-
ing of time you mature into understanding.

Job 28:28

28 Behold, the fear of the Lord, that is wisdom, and to depart from evil is understanding.

GOD'S CONDITIONAL PROMISES	RESPONSIBILITIES OF THE DOER OF THE WORD
1) Job 28:28	Job 28:28
28 Behold… …that is wisdom, and… …is understanding	28 (Behold) the fear of the Lord (that…) …(and) to depart from evil (is…)

There are three Conditional Promises God makes to us.

There are two responsibilities that we must do for God.

17 LIFE TOPIC   *Wisdom*

GOD'S CONDITIONAL PROMISES	RESPONSIBILITIES OF THE DOER OF THE WORD
1) Job 28:28	**Job 28:28**
28 Behold... ...that is wisdom, and... ...is understanding	28 (Behold) the fear of the Lord (that...) ...(and) to depart from evil (is...)
3) Ps. 37:30	**Ps. 37:30**
30 The mouth of... ...speaks wisdom	30 ...(of) the righteous (speaks...)
7) Prov. 3:6	**Prov. 3:5, 6**
      6 ...and He shall direct your paths	5 Trust in the Lord with all your heart ...lean not on your own understanding 6 ...in all your ways acknowledge Him (and...)
8) Prov. 3:13, 18	**Prov. 3:13, 18**
13 Happy is the man who... 18 She is a tree of life to those who... ...and happy are all who...	13 ...(who) finds wisdom ...(who) gains understanding 18 ...(who) take hold of her ...(who) retain her [hold her fast]

GOD'S CONDITIONAL PROMISES	RESPONSIBILITIES OF THE DOER OF THE WORD
11) Prov. 9:10	Prov. 9:10
10 ...is the beginning of wisdom and... ...is understanding	10 The fear of the Lord (is...) ...and the knowledge of the Holy One (is...)
12) Prov. 11:2	Prov. 11:2
2 ...when pride comes, then comes shame; but with... ...is wisdom	2 ...(with) the humble (is...)
13) Prov. 11:14	Prov. 11:14
14 ...there is safety	14 ...in the multitude of counselors (there...)
14) Prov. 12:8	Prov. 12:8
8 A man will be commended...	8 ...(commended) according to his wisdom
15) Prov. 13:10	Prov. 13:10
10 ...with the... ...is wisdom	10 ...(the) well-advised (is...)

17 LIFE TOPIC — *Wisdom*

GOD'S CONDITIONAL PROMISES	RESPONSIBILITIES OF THE DOER OF THE WORD
16) Prov. 13:15	**Prov. 13:15**
15 ...gains [gives] favor	15 Good understanding (gains...)
17) Prov. 14:6	**Prov. 14:6**
6 ...knowledge is easy to him who...	6 ...(who) understands
18) Prov. 14:18	**Prov. 14:18**
18 ...are crowned with knowledge	18 ...the prudent (are...)
22) Prov. 17:20	**Prov. 17:20**
20 He who... ...will be wise	20 ...(who) walks with wise men (will...)
23) Prov. 17:24	**Prov. 17:24**
24 Wisdom is in the sight of him who...	24 ...(who) has understanding
25) Prov. 20:15	**Prov. 20:15**
15 There is gold and a multitude of rubies, but... ...are a precious jewel	15 ...(but) the lips of knowledge (are...)
26) Prov. 21:11	**Prov. 21:11**
11 ...he receives knowledge	11 ...when the wise is instructed (he...)

Wisdom

GOD'S CONDITIONAL PROMISES	RESPONSIBILITIES OF THE DOER OF THE WORD
32) Eccl. 7:19	**Eccl. 7:19**
19 Wisdom strengthens… …more than ten rulers of the city	19 …(strengthens) the wise (more…)
34) Jer. 33:3	**Jer. 33:3**
3 …and I will answer you …(and I will) show you great…(things, which you do not know) …(and I will) show you mighty things, which you do not know	3 Call to Me (and…)
37) Matt. 12:35, 37	**Matt. 12:35, 37**
35 …out of the good treasure of his heart brings forth good things 37 …you will be justified	35 A good man (out…) 37 …by your words (you…)
44) John 8:47	**John 8:47**
47 He who… …hears God's words	47 …(who) is of God (hears…)
47) 1 Cor. 2:9	**1 Cor. 2:9**
9 Eye has not seen …nor ear heard …nor have entered into the heart of man the things which God has prepared for those who…	9 …(who) love Him

GOD'S CONDITIONAL PROMISES	RESPONSIBILITIES OF THE DOER OF THE WORD
55) 2 Tim. 2:7	2 Tim. 2:7
7 ...and may the Lord give you understanding in all things	7 Consider [heed] what I say (and...)
57) James 1:5	James 1:5, 6
5 If any of you lacks wisdom... ...who gives to all liberally ...and without reproach ...and it will be given to him	5 ...(wisdom) let him ask of God (who...) 6 but let him ask in faith ...with no doubting
59) 1 Pet. 2:2, 3	1 Pet. 2:1, 2, 3
2 ...that you may grow thereby 3 ...if...	1 ...laying aside all malice ...all deceit ...hypocrisy ...envy ...and all evil speaking 2 ...as newborn babes, desire the pure milk of the word (that...) 3 ...(if) indeed you have tasted that the Lord is gracious

Wisdom

LIFE TOPIC 17

GOD'S CONDITIONAL PROMISES	RESPONSIBILITIES OF THE DOER OF THE WORD
61) Rev. 1:3	**Rev. 1:3**
3 Blessed is he who… …and those who… …for the time is near	3 …(who) reads …(who) hear the words of this prophecy …and keep those things which are written in it (for…)

LIFE
TOPIC 18

Children and Youth

Temptation and adversity; sharing, overcoming, and encouraging others

Nothing is more precious and valuable than the faith, hope, trust, and love that pour out of the hearts and minds of youngsters. Walking closely with Jesus while you are young is the key so that as you eventually grow older in body, you can remain young in heart and in mind. "I have come that they may have life, and that they may have it more abundantly" (John 10:10, NKJV).

Psalm 115:13

13 He will bless those who fear the
Lord, both small and great.

	GOD'S CONDITIONAL PROMISES		RESPONSIBILITIES OF THE DOER OF THE WORD
	2) Ps. 115:13		Ps. 115:13
13	He will bless those who...	13	...(who) fear the Lord (both...)
	...both small and great [that are young in age]		

There are two Conditional Promises God makes to us.

There is one responsibility that we must do for God.

18 LIFE TOPIC — *Children and Youth*

GOD'S CONDITIONAL PROMISES	RESPONSIBILITIES OF THE DOER OF THE WORD
2) Ps. 115:13	**Ps. 115:13**
13 He will bless those who... ...both small and great [that are young in age]	13 ...(who) fear the Lord (both...)
7) Prov. 14:22	**Prov. 14:22**
22 ...mercy and truth belong to those who...	22 ...(who) devise good
9) Prov. 15:5	**Prov. 15:5**
5 ...he who... ...is prudent	5 ...(who) receives [keeps] correction (is...)
10) Prov. 16:17	**Prov. 16:17**
17 ...he who... ...preserves his soul	17 ...(who) keeps his way (preserves...)
12) Prov. 19:20	**Prov. 19:20**
20 ...that you may be wise in your latter days	20 Listen to counsel ...and receive instruction (that...)
13) Prov. 20:11	**Prov. 20:11**
11 Even a child is known by his deeds...	11 ...(deeds) whether what he does is pure and right

Children and Youth LIFE TOPIC 18

GOD'S CONDITIONAL PROMISES	RESPONSIBILITIES OF THE DOER OF THE WORD
14) Prov. 20:29	**Prov. 20:29**
29 The glory of young men is...	29 ...(is) their strength
16) Eccl. 7:12	**Eccl. 7:12**
12 ...the excellence [advantage or profit] of knowledge is that wisdom gives life to those who...	12 ...(who) have it [knowledge]
21) Matt. 23:12	**Matt. 23:12**
12 ...he who ...will be exalted	12 ...(who) humbles himself (will...)
23) Luke 11:28	**Luke 11:28**
28 ...blessed are those who...	28 ...(who) hear the word of God ...and (who) keep it
26) Rom. 8:28	**Rom. 8:28**
28 And we know that all things work together for good to those who... ...to those who... ...according to His purpose	28 ...(who) love God ...(who) are the called (according...)

18 LIFE TOPIC   *Children and Youth*

GOD'S CONDITIONAL PROMISES	RESPONSIBILITIES OF THE DOER OF THE WORD
27) Eph. 6:1, 3	**Eph. 6:1, 2**
1 …for this is right 3 …that it may be well with you …and you may live long on the earth	1 Children, obey your parents in the Lord (for…) 2 Honor your father …and (honor your) mother
28) Col. 3:20	**Col. 3:20**
20 …this is well pleasing to the Lord	20 Children, obey your parents in all things for (this…)
32) 1 Pet. 5:5	**1 Pet. 5:5**
5 …you younger people… …God resists the proud …but gives grace to…	5 …(people) submit yourselves to your elders …be submissive to one another …be clothed with humility …(to) the humble

GOD'S CONDITIONAL PROMISES	RESPONSIBILITIES OF THE DOER OF THE WORD
34.4) Prov. 1:9	Prov. 1:8
	8 …hear the instruction of your father …do not forsake the law of your mother
9 …for they (the instruction of your father) will be a graceful ornament on your head …and (the law of your mother) (will be) chains about your neck	
Symbolic Commentary	

If the young doer of the Word will receive and follow the instruction of his parents with a positive and willing heart, his obedience will be turned into substantial blessings. He will become wise and others will take notice of his wisdom and find favor in him. God does not want the doer of the Word to think of parental guidance and instruction as a burden or negative "don'ts."

LIFE 19
TOPIC

Eternal Life

Assurance you are saved by Jesus Christ

Life is short, and eternity is forever. Picture this — a string has been tied from the top of the tallest building in New York City to the top of the tallest building in Los Angeles. At the beginning point on that sting a very tiny dot is made with a pen. That dot represents the entire span of a life on earth. The rest of the string represents eternity (although eternity really has no end). Jesus knows each person who has put his trust in Him, and who will be spending all of that time (the string) with Him, when their life (the dot) has reached its end. That's an assurance you want to have.

Psalm 149:4

4 For the Lord takes pleasure in His people; He will beautify the humble with salvation.

GOD'S CONDITIONAL PROMISES	RESPONSIBILITIES OF THE DOER OF THE WORD
2) Ps. 149:4	Ps. 149:4
4 …the Lord takes pleasure in… …He will beautify… …with salvation	4 …(in) His people (He…) …(beautify) the humble (with…)

There are three Conditional Promises God makes to us.

There are two responsibilities that we must do for God.

GOD'S CONDITIONAL PROMISES	RESPONSIBILITIES OF THE DOER OF THE WORD
2) Ps. 149:4	Ps. 149:4
4 ...the Lord takes pleasure in... ...He will beautify... ...with salvation	4 ...(in) His people (He...) ...(beautify) the humble (with...)
3) Prov. 10:2	Prov. 10:2
2 ... delivers from death [separation from God]	2 ... righteousness [characteristic of the truly wise] (delivers...)
4) Prov. 19:16	Prov. 19:16
16 He who... ...keeps his soul	16 ...(who) keeps the commandments (keeps...)
10) Nah. 1:7	Nah. 1:7
7 ...The Lord is good ...and He knows those who...	7 ...(who) trust in Him
11) Zech. 2:10	Zech. 2:10
10 ...I am coming ...and I will dwell in your midst	10 Sing and rejoice...

GOD'S CONDITIONAL PROMISES	RESPONSIBILITIES OF THE DOER OF THE WORD
14) Matt. 5:19	Matt. 5:19
19 ...but whoever... ...he shall be called great in the kingdom of heaven	19 ...(whoever) does ...and (whoever) teaches them (he...)
15) Matt. 13:43	Matt. 13:43
43 ...will shine forth as the sun in the kingdom of their Father	43 ...the righteous (will...)
16) Mark 2:27	Mark 2:27
27 The Sabbath was made for man, and not man for the Sabbath	27 ...have you never read [the Scriptures]
18) Luke 8:21	Luke 8:21
21 My mother ...and My brothers are these who...	21 ...(who) hear the word of God ...and do it (the word of God)

19 LIFE TOPIC — *Eternal Life*

GOD'S CONDITIONAL PROMISES	RESPONSIBILITIES OF THE DOER OF THE WORD
33) 2 Cor. 13:5	**2 Cor. 13:5**
5 ...Do you not know yourselves, that Jesus Christ is in you? ...unless indeed you are disqualified	5 Examine yourselves as to whether you are in the faith Test yourselves (Do...)
50) Heb. 12:2	**Heb. 12:1, 2**
2 ...the author and finisher of our faith	1 ...lay aside every weight ...and (lay aside) the sin which so easily ensnares us ...and let us run with endurance the race that is set before us 2 ...looking unto Jesus (the...)
54) 1 John 1:7	**1 John 1:7**
7 ...if... ...the blood of Jesus Christ His Son cleanses us from all sin	7 ...(if) we walk in the light as He is in the light (the...)

GOD'S CONDITIONAL PROMISES	RESPONSIBILITIES OF THE DOER OF THE WORD
57) 1 John 2:29	**1 John 2:29**
29 If... ...that everyone who... ...is born of Him	29 (If) you know that He is righteous ...you know (that...) ...(who) practices righteousness (is...)
61) 2 John 9	**2 John 9**
9 He who... ...has both the Father ...and the Son	9 ...(who) abides in the doctrine of Christ (has...)

LIFE TOPIC 20

Fasting

According to God's standards and directions

There are benefits when fasting for health, but fasting for God takes on a totally different design. It becomes a way to express to God your seriousness about a matter, your resolve in a situation, a way of pleading for an answer from God, or an entreaty that He would show you the answer He wants. It is personal and passionate in every way. It is prompted by God's leading, because there is a time and place where He wants to meet you. All of this should be done in humble privacy — not with boasting.

Matthew 6:17, 18

17 But you, when you fast, anoint your head and wash your face,

18 so that you do not appear to men to be fasting, but to your Father who is in the secret place; and your Father who sees in secret will reward you openly.

GOD'S CONDITIONAL PROMISES	RESPONSIBILITIES OF THE DOER OF THE WORD
2) Matt. 6:17, 18	Matt. 6:17, 18
17 …when you fast…	17 …(fast) anoint your head …and wash your face 18 so that you do not appear to men to be fasting, but to your Father who is in the secret place (and…)
18 …and your Father who sees in secret will reward you openly	

There are two Conditional Promises God makes to us. There are three responsibilities that we must do for God.

GOD'S CONDITIONAL PROMISES	RESPONSIBILITIES OF THE DOER OF THE WORD
2) Matt. 6:17, 18	Matt. 6:17, 18
17 ...when you fast...	17 ...(fast) anoint your head ...and wash your face 18 so that you do not appear to men to be fasting, but to your Father who is in the secret place (and...)
18 ...and your Father who sees in secret will reward you openly	

Reflection Notes

LIFE TOPIC 21

Salvation

Believing on Jesus Christ
alone for eternal life

In the Bible, only *one Conditional Promise of God Life Topic* is available to a person who has not repented of his sins, believed that the blood of Jesus Christ on the cross has paid for his sins, and has made a true profession of faith that Jesus Christ is his personal savior. *This* is the *only Conditional Promise Life Topic* you have — until you become born again by the Spirit of God.

Matthew 4:19

19 Follow Me, and I will make you
fishers of men.

GOD'S CONDITIONAL PROMISES	RESPONSIBILITIES OF THE DOER OF THE WORD
5) Matt. 4:19	Matt. 4:19
19 ...and I will make you fishers of men	19 ...follow Me, (and...)

There is one Conditional Promise God makes to us.

There is one responsibility that we must do for God.

GOD'S CONDITIONAL PROMISES	RESPONSIBILITIES OF THE DOER OF THE WORD
5) Matt. 4:19	Matt. 4:19
19 ...and I will make you fishers of men	19 ...follow Me, (and...)
7) Matt. 10:40	Matt. 10:40
40 He who receives you receives Me, and he who... ...receives Him who sent Me	40 ...(who) receives Me (receives...)
10) Matt. 19:29	Matt. 19:29
29 ...everyone who... ...shall receive a hundredfold ...and inherit eternal life	29 ...(who) has left houses ...(who) has left brothers ...(who) has left sisters ... ...(who) has left father ...(who) has left mother ...(who) has left wife ...(who) has left children ...(who) has left lands, for My name's sake (shall...)
12) Mark 2:17	Mark 2:17
17 I did not come to call the righteous, but sinners...	17 ...(sinners) to repentance

GOD'S CONDITIONAL PROMISES	RESPONSIBILITIES OF THE DOER OF THE WORD
17) Luke 7:23	**Luke 7:23**
23 And blessed is he who...	23 ...(who) is not offended because of Me
18) Luke 12:8	**Luke 12:8**
8 ...whoever ...him the Son of Man also will confess before the angels of God	8 ...(whoever) confesses Me before men (him...)
21) John 1:12, 13	**John 1:12, 13**
12 But as many as... ...to them He gave the right [authority] to become children of God ...to those who... 13 ...who were born, not of blood, nor of the will of the flesh, nor of the will of man, but (who)...	12 ...(as) received Him (to...) ...(who) believe in His name 13 ...(who were born) of God
23) John 5:24	**John 5:24**
24 ...he who... ...has everlasting life ...and shall not come into judgment ...but has passed from death into life	24 ...(who) hears My word ...and believes in Him who sent Me (has...)

21 LIFE TOPIC   *Salvation*

GOD'S CONDITIONAL PROMISES	RESPONSIBILITIES OF THE DOER OF THE WORD
24) John 6:47	**John 6:47**
47 Most assuredly, I say to you, he who… …has everlasting life	47 …(who) believes in Me (has…)
26) John 8:12	**John 8:12**
12 I am the light of the world. He who… …shall not walk in darkness …but have the light of life	12 …(who) follows Me (shall…)
28) John 11:25, 26	**John 11:25, 26**
25 I am the resurrection and the life. He who… …though he may die, he shall live 26 …whoever… …shall never die	25 …(who) believes in Me (though…) 26 …(whoever) lives …and believes in Me (shall…)

Salvation

LIFE TOPIC 21

GOD'S CONDITIONAL PROMISES	RESPONSIBILITIES OF THE DOER OF THE WORD
29) John 14:6, 7, 9	John 14:7, 9, 11
6 I am the way, the truth, and the life. No one comes to the Father except through Me.	
7 If…	7 (If) you had known Me (you…)
…you would have known My Father also …and from now on you know Him and have seen Him	
9 He who…	9 …(who) has seen Me (has…)
…has seen the Father	11 Believe Me that I am in the Father and the Father in Me …or else believe Me for the sake of the works themselves
31) Acts 2:21	Acts 2:21
21 …it shall come to pass that whoever…	21 …(whoever) calls on the name of the Lord
…shall be saved	
33) Acts 4:10, 12	Acts 4:12
10 …by the name of Jesus Christ of Nazareth	
12 …for there is no other name under heaven given among men by which…	12 …(which) we must be saved

21 LIFE TOPIC   *Salvation*

GOD'S CONDITIONAL PROMISES	RESPONSIBILITIES OF THE DOER OF THE WORD
35) Acts 16:31	Acts 16:31
31 ...you will be saved ...you and your household	31 ...believe on the Lord Jesus Christ (and...)
44) 1 Thess. 2:12	1 Thess. 2:12
12 ...who calls you into His own kingdom and glory	12 ...walk worthy of God (who...)
45) 1 Tim. 4:10	1 Tim. 4:10
10 ...who is the Savior of all men ...especially of those who...	10 ...trust in the living God (who...) ...(who) believe
48) Heb. 7:25	Heb. 7:25
25 He is also able to save to the uttermost those who... ...since He always lives to make intercession for them	25 ...(who) come to God through Him (since...)

GOD'S CONDITIONAL PROMISES	RESPONSIBILITIES OF THE DOER OF THE WORD
51) 2 Pet. 3:9	**2 Pet. 3:9**
9 ...the Lord is not slack concerning His promise, as some count slackness ...but (the Lord) is longsuffering toward us ...(the Lord is) not willing that any should perish ...but that all...	9 ...(all) should come to repentance

LIFE TOPIC 22

Trials and Temptations

Emerging the victor

Trials are for building up your most holy faith. Temptations are allowed by God as opportunities to release and apply your most holy faith and prayer in the Holy Spirit (Jude 20). Each time you overcome any temptation, you continue living in victorious communion with Jesus Christ.

Proverbs 15:27

27 But he who hates bribes will live.

GOD'S CONDITIONAL PROMISES	RESPONSIBILITIES OF THE DOER OF THE WORD
2) Prov. 15:27	Prov. 15:27
27 ...he who... ...will live	27 ...(who) hates bribes (will...)

There are two Conditional Promises God makes to us. There is one responsibility that we must do for God.

22 LIFE TOPIC *Trials and Temptations*

GOD'S CONDITIONAL PROMISES	RESPONSIBILITIES OF THE DOER OF THE WORD
2) Prov. 15:27	**Prov. 15:27**
27 ...he who... ...will live	27 ...(who) hates bribes (will...)
3) Isa. 57:1	**Isa. 57:1**
1 ...is taken away from [the face of] evil	1 ...the righteous (is...)
4) Matt. 26:41	**Matt. 26:41**
41 ...lest you enter into temptation	41 Watch ...and pray (lest...)
7) 1 Cor. 6:19, 20	**1 Cor. 6:20**
19 ...your body is the temple of the Holy Spirit who is in you ...whom you have from God ...and you are not your own 20 ...you were bought at a price; therefore... ...which are God's	20 ...(therefore) glorify God in your body ...and (glorify God) in your spirit (which...)

GOD'S CONDITIONAL PROMISES	RESPONSIBILITIES OF THE DOER OF THE WORD
9) 1 Cor. 15:33, 34	**1 Cor. 15:33, 34**
33 ...Evil company corrupts good habits 34 ...for some do not have the knowledge of God	33 Do not be deceived (Evil...) 34 Awake to righteousness ...and do not sin (for...)
19) 2 Pet. 2:9	**2 Pet. 2:9**
9 ...the Lord knows how to deliver... ...out of temptations	9 ...(deliver) the godly (out...)
21) 1 John 5:18	**1 John 5:18, 21**
18 We know that whoever... ...does not sin but he who... ...and the wicked one does not touch him	18 ...(whoever) is born of God (does...) ...(who) has been born of God keeps himself (and...) 21 ...keep yourselves from idols

LIFE TOPIC 23

Repentance

After giving in to temptation

True repentance is a change of mind and heart — that results in a change of actions and direction. The repentant thief says, "I am so sorry for having stolen." The unrepentant heart says, "I am so sorry I got caught."

Proverbs 28:13

13 But whoever confesses and for-
sakes them will have mercy.

GOD'S CONDITIONAL PROMISES	RESPONSIBILITIES OF THE DOER OF THE WORD
2) Prov. 28:13	Prov. 28:13
	13 ...whoever confesses (his sins) ...and (whoever) forsakes (his sins) (will...)
13 ...will have mercy	

There is one Conditional Promise God makes to us.

There are two responsibilities that we must do for God.

23 LIFE TOPIC — *Repentance*

GOD'S CONDITIONAL PROMISES	RESPONSIBILITIES OF THE DOER OF THE WORD
2) Prov. 28:13	**Prov. 28:13**
	13 ...whoever confesses (his sins) ...and (whoever) forsakes (his sins) (will...)
13 ...will have mercy	
5) Matt. 4:17	**Matt. 4:17**
	17 ...repent [a decision that results in a change of thinking and direction] (for...)
17 ...for the kingdom of heaven is at hand [has drawn near]	
6) Luke 8:17, 18	**Luke 8:18**
17 ...nothing is secret that will not be revealed ...nor anything hidden that will not be known and come to light 18 For whoever... ...to him more will be given	18 ...take heed how you hear ...(whoever) has (to...)

Repentance

LIFE TOPIC 23

GOD'S CONDITIONAL PROMISES	RESPONSIBILITIES OF THE DOER OF THE WORD
7) Luke 15:7, 10	Luke 15:7, 10
7 ...there will be more joy in heaven over one sinner who... ...than over ninety-nine just persons who need no repentance 10 ...there is joy in the presence of the angels of God over one sinner who...	7 ...(who) repents (than...) 10 ...(who) repents
9) Heb. 4:16	Heb. 4:16
16 ...that we may obtain mercy ...and find grace to help in time of need	16 ...come boldly to the throne of grace (that...)
11) 1 John 1:9	1 John 1:9
9 If... ...He is faithful (to forgive us our sins) ...and just to forgive us our sins ...and to cleanse us from all unrighteousness	9 (If) we confess our sins (He...)

LIFE TOPIC 24

Prayer

Asking, believing, and speaking by faith in Christ

True prayer is an ongoing, open conversation with God our Father through the power of the Holy Spirit in the name of Jesus Christ our LORD. It should start when you wake up, interlace throughout everything that takes place all day, and pause when you fall asleep — only to be picked up again first thing the next morning. It's having your best friend, God, around all the time.

Matthew 6:6, 7

6 But you, when you pray, go into your room, and when you have shut your door, pray to your Father who is in the secret place; and your Father who sees in secret will reward you openly.

7 And when you pray, do not use vain repetitions as the heathen do.

GOD'S CONDITIONAL PROMISES	RESPONSIBILITIES OF THE DOER OF THE WORD
2) Matt. 6:6	**Matt. 6:6, 7**
6 …when you pray…	6 …(pray) go into your room, and when you have shut your door, pray to your Father who is in the secret place (and…)
…and your Father who sees in secret will reward you openly	7 And when you pray do not use vain repetitions as the heathen do

There are two Conditional Promises God makes to us.
There are two responsibilities that we must do for God.

24 LIFE TOPIC *Prayer*

GOD'S CONDITIONAL PROMISES	RESPONSIBILITIES OF THE DOER OF THE WORD
2) Matt. 6:6	Matt. 6:6, 7
6 …when you pray… …and your Father who sees in secret will reward you openly	6 …(pray) go into your room, and when you have shut your door, pray to your Father who is in the secret place (and…) 7 And when you pray do not use vain repetitions as the heathen do
4) Matt. 16:19	Matt. 16:19
19 …I will give you the keys of the kingdom of heaven, and whatever… …(on earth) will be [will have been] bound in heaven …(on earth) will be [will have been] loosed in heaven	19 …(whatever) you bind [declare to be improper and unlawful] on earth… …and whatever you loose [declare lawful] on earth…
5) Matt. 17:20	Matt. 17:20
20 …if… …and it will move …and nothing will be impossible for you	20 …(if) you have faith as a mustard seed, you will say to this mountain, Move from here to there (and…)

GOD'S CONDITIONAL PROMISES	RESPONSIBILITIES OF THE DOER OF THE WORD
6) Matt. 18:18, 19, 20	**Matt. 18:18, 19, 20**
18 ...whatever...	18 ...(whatever) you bind [declare to be improper and unlawful] on earth (will...)
...will be [will have been] bound in heaven ...whatever	...(whatever) you loose [declare lawful] on earth (will...)
...will be [will have been] loosed in heaven 19 ...if...	19 ...(if) two of you agree on earth concerning anything that they ask (it...)
...it will be done for them by My Father in heaven 20 For where...	20 ...(where) two or three are gathered together in My name (I...)
...I am there in the midst of them	
7) Matt. 21:21, 22	**Matt. 21:21, 22**
21 ...if...	21 ...(if) you have faith ...and (if you) do not doubt ...you say to this mountain, Be removed and be cast into the sea (it...)
...it will be done 22 ...whatever things...	22 ...(things) you ask in prayer, believing (you...)
...you will receive	

24 LIFE TOPIC   *Prayer*

GOD'S CONDITIONAL PROMISES	RESPONSIBILITIES OF THE DOER OF THE WORD
9) Luke 11:9, 10, 13	Luke 11:9, 10, 13
9 ...and it will be given to you ...and you will find ...and it will be opened to you 10 For everyone who... ...receives ...and he who... ...finds ...and to him who... ...it will be opened 13 If you then, being evil, know how to give good gifts to your children, how much more will your heavenly Father give the Holy Spirit to those who...	9 ...ask (and it...) ...seek (and you...) ...knock (and it...) 10 ...(who) asks... ...(who) seeks... ...(who) knocks... 13 ...(who) ask Him
11) John 15:7	John 15:7
7 If you... ...you will... ...and it shall be done for you	7 (If) you abide in Me ...and My words abide in you (you...) ...(will) ask what you desire (and...)

GOD'S CONDITIONAL PROMISES	RESPONSIBILITIES OF THE DOER OF THE WORD
13) Phil. 4:7	Phil. 4:6
7 …and the peace of God, which surpasses all understanding, will guard your hearts …and (will guard your) minds through Christ Jesus	6 Be anxious for nothing …but in everything by prayer …and supplication …with thanksgiving let your requests be made known to God (and…)
14) 1 Thess. 5:18, 24	1 Thess. 5:17
18 …this is the will of God in Christ Jesus for you 24 …He who calls you is faithful …who also will do it [sanctify you completely]	17 …pray without ceasing

24 LIFE TOPIC   *Prayer*

GOD'S CONDITIONAL PROMISES	RESPONSIBILITIES OF THE DOER OF THE WORD
15) James 5:14, 15, 16	**James 5:14, 15, 16**
14 Is anyone among you sick	14 Let him call for the elders of the church ...and let them pray over him ...anointing him with oil in the name of the Lord
15 And the...	15 ...(the) prayer of faith (will...)
...will save the sick ...and the Lord will raise him up ...if he has committed sins, he will be forgiven	
	16 Confess your trespasses to one another ...and pray for one another (that...)
16 ...that you may be healed	The effective (prayer) ...(the) fervent prayer of a righteous man (avails...)
...avails much	
16) 1 Pet. 3:7	**1 Pet. 3:7**
	7 Husbands, likewise, dwell with them with understanding ... giving honor to the wife, as to the weaker vessel ...and as being heirs together of the grace of life (that...)
7 ...that your prayers may not be hindered	

Prayer

GOD'S CONDITIONAL PROMISES	RESPONSIBILITIES OF THE DOER OF THE WORD
17) 1 Pet. 3:12	1 Pet. 3:12
12 For the eyes of the Lord are on the... ...and His ears are open to their...	12 ...(the) righteous ...(their) prayers
19) 1 John 5:14, 15	1 John 5:14, 15
14 Now this is the confidence that we have in Him, that if... ...He hears us 15 And if... ...whatever we ask...	14 ...(if) we ask anything according to His will (He...) 15 ...(if) we know that He hears us (whatever...) ...(ask) we know that we have the petitions that we have asked of Him

GOD'S CONDITIONAL PROMISES	RESPONSIBILITIES OF THE DOER OF THE WORD
21.4) John 14:13, 14	John 14:13, 14
13 ...whatever... ...that I will do ...that the Father may be glorified in the Son 14 If... ...I will do it.	13 ...(whatever) you ask in My name (that...) 14 (If) you ask anything in My name (I...)
Symbolic Commentary	
"In my name" means that when the doer of the Word prays with the character, nature, personality, and known will of Jesus, according to His word; then Jesus will act on that prayer so that the Father will be glorified.	

GOD'S CONDITIONAL PROMISES	RESPONSIBILITIES OF THE DOER OF THE WORD
22.4) John 16:23, 24, 25, 26, 27	John 16:23, 24, 26, 27
23 And in that day you will ask Me nothing. Most assuredly, I say to you, whatever…	
	23 …(whatever) you ask the Father in My name (He…)
…He will give you	
24 Until now you have asked nothing in My name …and you will receive …that your joy may be full	24 Ask (and…)
25 …the time is coming when I will no longer speak to you in figurative language, but I will tell you plainly about the Father	
26 In that day you will…	26 …(will) ask in My name
27 …for the Father Himself loves you, because…	27 …(because) you have loved Me …and have believed that I came forth from God
Symbolic Commentary	

It is the Holy Spirit who increases our knowledge of spiritual things. Through Him, the prayer life of the doer of the Word is enhanced and empowered. Asking anything in the name of Jesus means the request must be aligned with His character, nature, and personality.

LIFE TOPIC 25

Preaching the Gospel

Experiencing resistance, opposition,
and the Holy Spirit's power

Preach the Gospel at all times.
When necessary, use words.

It is no use walking anywhere to preach,
unless our walking is our preaching.

Saint Francis of Assisi
1181 - 1226

Matthew 28:19, 20

19 Go therefore and make disciples
of all the nations, baptizing them
in the name of the Father and of
the Son and of the Holy Spirit,

20 teaching them to observe all
things that I have commanded
you; and lo, I am with you always,
even to the end of the age.

GOD'S CONDITIONAL PROMISES	RESPONSIBILITIES OF THE DOER OF THE WORD
3) Matt. 28:20	Matt. 28:19, 20
	19 Go therefore and make disciples of all the nations …baptizing them in the name of the Father …and (baptizing them in the name) of the Son …and (baptizing them in the name) of the Holy Spirit
	20 …teaching them to observe all things that I have commanded you (and…)
20 …and lo, I am with you always, even to the end of the age	

There is one Conditional Promise God makes to us.

There are five responsibilities that we must do for God.

25 **LIFE TOPIC** *Preaching the Gospel*

GOD'S CONDITIONAL PROMISES	RESPONSIBILITIES OF THE DOER OF THE WORD
3) Matt. 28:20	Matt. 28:19, 20
	19 Go therefore and make disciples of all the nations ...baptizing them in the name of the Father ...and (baptizing them in the name) of the Son ...and (baptizing them in the name) of the Holy Spirit 20 ...teaching them to observe all things that I have commanded you (and...)
20 ...and lo, I am with you always, even to the end of the age	

GOD'S CONDITIONAL PROMISES	RESPONSIBILITIES OF THE DOER OF THE WORD
4) Mark 16:16, 17, 18	**Mark 16:15, 16, 17**
	15 Go into all the world and preach the gospel to every creature
16 He who…	16 …(who) believes …and is baptized (will…)
…will be saved	
17 And these signs will follow those who… …In My name they will cast out demons …they will speak with new tongues	17 …(who) believe: (In…)
18 …they will take up [remove, take away, cast away] serpents …and if they drink anything deadly, it will by no means hurt them …they will lay hands on the sick, and they will recover	
5) Luke 5:10	**Luke 5:10**
	10 Do not be afraid
10 From now on you will catch men [win souls for Jesus]	

GOD'S CONDITIONAL PROMISES	RESPONSIBILITIES OF THE DOER OF THE WORD
7) John 12:32, 36	John 12:32, 35, 36
32 And I, when… …[I] will draw all peoples to Myself 36 While you have the light… …that you may become sons of light	32 …(when) I am lifted up from the earth [I] (will…) 35 Walk while you have the light 36 …(light) believe in the light (that…)
9) Rom. 10:15	Rom. 10:15
15 How beautiful are the feet of those who… …who…	15 …(who) preach the gospel of peace …(who) bring glad tidings of good things
15) Col. 4:6	Col. 4:2, 5, 6
        6 …that you may know how you ought to answer each one	2 Continue earnestly in prayer …being vigilant in it with thanksgiving 5 Walk in wisdom toward those who are outside …redeeming the time 6 Let your speech always be with grace …seasoned with salt (that…)

GOD'S CONDITIONAL PROMISES	RESPONSIBILITIES OF THE DOER OF THE WORD
17) 2 Tim. 2:9, 10	**2 Tim. 2:10**
9 ...the word of God is not chained 10 ...that they also may obtain the salvation which is in Christ Jesus with eternal glory	10 ...I endure all things for the sake of the elect (that...)
22) 1 John 4:2, 4, 6	**1 John 4:2, 6**
2 By this you know the Spirit of God: Every spirit that... ...is of God 4 You are of God, little children, and have overcome them, because He who is in you is greater than he who is in the world 6 He who... ...hears [understands and receives] us ...By this we know the spirit of truth ...and the spirit of error	2 ...(that) confesses that Jesus Christ has come in the flesh (is...) 6 ...(who) knows God (hears...)

LIFE TOPIC 26

Sins or Offenses

Committed between believers

Nothing makes two parents happier than to watch each of their children playing together and being kind toward on another. Why would God, as our loving heavenly Father, feel or respond any differently? "Therefore be imitators of God as dear children. And walk in love, as Christ also has loved us and given Himself for us, an offering and a sacrifice to God for a sweet-smelling aroma" (Ephesians 5:1, 2, NKJV).

Luke 6:42

42 First remove the plank from your own eye, and then you will see clearly to remove the speck that is in your brother's eye.

GOD'S CONDITIONAL PROMISES	RESPONSIBILITIES OF THE DOER OF THE WORD
4) Luke 6:42	Luke 6:42
	42 First remove the plank from your own eye (and...)
42 ...and then you will see clearly to remove the speck that is in your brother's eye	

There is one Conditional Promise God makes to us.

There is one responsibility that we must do for God.

26 LIFE TOPIC — *Sins or Offenses*

GOD'S CONDITIONAL PROMISES	RESPONSIBILITIES OF THE DOER OF THE WORD
4) Luke 6:42	**Luke 6:42**
42 ...and then you will see clearly to remove the speck that is in your brother's eye	42 First remove the plank from your own eye (and...)
7) John 13:34, 35	**John 13:34, 35**
34 A new commandment I give to you... 35 By this all will know that you are My disciples, if...	34 ...(you) that you love one another ...as I have loved you ...that you also love one another 35 ...(if) you have love for one another
9) Rom. 15:7	**Rom. 15:7**
7 ...to the glory of God	7 ...receive one another, just as Christ also received us (to...)
27) 1 John 1:7	**1 John 1:7**
7 ...if... ...we have fellowship with one another	7 ...(if) we walk in the light as He is in the light (we...)

GOD'S CONDITIONAL PROMISES	RESPONSIBILITIES OF THE DOER OF THE WORD
28) 1 John 2:10	**1 John 2:10**
10 He who... ...abides in the light ...and there is no cause for stumbling in him	10 ...(who) loves his brother (abides...)
29) 1 John 5:1	**1 John 5:1**
1 Whoever... ...is born of God ...and everyone who... ...also loves him [fellow believers] who is begotten of Him	1 (Whoever) believes that Jesus is the Christ (is...) ...(who) loves Him who begot (also...)

LIFE TOPIC 27

The Return of Jesus

The end times, judgment, and rewards

There is no outstanding prophecy to be fulfilled before Jesus returns for His church. The last one was fulfilled in 1948 when Israel became a nation. Jesus can come today. If God woke you up this morning, He's obviously not finished with you yet. Spend your time serving others, and seeking His purpose for waking you today.

27 For the Son of Man will come in
the glory of His Father with His
angels, and then He will reward
each according to his works.

	GOD'S CONDITIONAL PROMISES	RESPONSIBILITIES OF THE DOER OF THE WORD
	2) Matt. 16:27	Matt. 16:27
27	For the Son of Man will come in the glory of His Father with His angels, and then He will reward each according to...	
		27 ...(to) his works

There one Conditional Promise God makes to us.

There is one responsibility that we must do for God.

27 LIFE TOPIC *The Return of Jesus*

GOD'S CONDITIONAL PROMISES	RESPONSIBILITIES OF THE DOER OF THE WORD
2) Matt. 16:27	**Matt. 16:27**
27 For the Son of Man will come in the glory of His Father with His angels, and then He will reward each according to…	27 …(to) his works
3) Matt. 24:13	**Matt. 24:4, 13**
13 …he who …shall be saved	4 Take heed that no one deceives you 13 …(who) endures to the end (shall…)
4) Matt. 24:46, 47	**Matt. 24:46**
46 Blessed is that servant whom his master, when he comes, will find… 47 Assuredly, I say to you that he will make him ruler over all his goods	46 …(find) (that servant) so doing
7) Mark 13:13	**Mark 13:13, 33, 37**
13 …he who …shall be saved	13 …(who) endures to the end (shall…) 33 Take heed …watch …and pray; for you do not know when the time is 37 Watch

The Return of Jesus LIFE TOPIC 27

GOD'S CONDITIONAL PROMISES	RESPONSIBILITIES OF THE DOER OF THE WORD
9) Luke 14:14	**Luke 14:13**
	13 ...invite the poor ...(invite) the maimed [disabled] ...(invite) the lame ...(invite) the blind
14 ...you will be blessed, because they cannot repay you ...for you shall be repaid at the resurrection of the just	
11) John 5:25	**John 5:25**
25 Most assuredly, I say to you, the hour is coming, and now is, when the dead will hear the voice of the Son of God; and those who... ...will live	25 ...(who) hear (will...)
12) John 14:2, 3	**John 14:1**
	1 Let not your heart be troubled ...you believe in God ...believe also in Me
2 In My Father's house are many mansions; if it were not so, I would have told you. I go to prepare a place for you. 3 And if I go and prepare a place for you, I will come again and receive you to Myself; that where I am, there you may be also	

27 LIFE TOPIC — *The Return of Jesus*

GOD'S CONDITIONAL PROMISES	RESPONSIBILITIES OF THE DOER OF THE WORD
14) 1 Cor. 1:8	**1 Cor. 1:7**
8 ...who will also confirm you to the end ...that you may be blameless in the day of our Lord Jesus Christ	7 ...eagerly waiting for the revelation of our Lord Jesus Christ
19) 1 Cor. 15:22, 23, 24	**1 Cor. 15:22, 23**
22 ...all shall be made alive 23 But each one in his own order ...Christ the firstfruits ...afterward those who... 24 Then comes the end, when He delivers the kingdom to God the Father, when He puts an end to all rule and all authority and power	22 ...in Christ (all...) 23 ... (who) are Christ's at His coming

GOD'S CONDITIONAL PROMISES	RESPONSIBILITIES OF THE DOER OF THE WORD
21) Phil. 3:20, 21	Phil. 3:20; 4:1
20 ...our citizenship is in heaven, from which...	20 ...(which) we also eagerly wait for the Savior, the Lord Jesus Christ (who...)
21 ...who will transform our lowly body ...that it may be conformed to His glorious body ...according to the working by which He is able even to subdue all things to Himself	1 ...so stand fast in the Lord
23) 1 Thess. 4:14, 16	1 Thess. 4:14, 18
14 ...if...	14 ...(if) we believe that Jesus died ...and (believe that Jesus) rose again (even...)
...even so God will bring with Him those who sleep in Jesus 16 ...the Lord Himself will descend from heaven with a shout ...with the voice of an archangel ...and with the trumpet of God ...the dead in Christ will rise first	18 ...comfort one another with these words

GOD'S CONDITIONAL PROMISES	RESPONSIBILITIES OF THE DOER OF THE WORD
24) 2 Thess. 1:10	2 Thess. 1:10
10 ...when He comes, in that Day, to be glorified in His saints ...and to be admired among all those who...	10 ...(who) believe
26) 2 Tim. 4:8	2 Tim. 4:8
8 ...the crown of righteousness, which the Lord, the righteous Judge, will give to me on that Day ...and not to me only but also to all who...	8 ...(who) have loved His appearing
27) Heb. 9:28	Heb. 9:28
28 To those who... ...He will appear a second time ...apart from sin ...for salvation	28 ...(who) eagerly wait for Him (He...)
28) James 5:8	James 5:8
8 ...for the coming of the Lord is at hand	8 You also be patient Establish your hearts (for...)

GOD'S CONDITIONAL PROMISES	RESPONSIBILITIES OF THE DOER OF THE WORD
33) 1 John 2:28	1 John 2:28
28 ...that when He appears ...we may have confidence ...and not be ashamed before Him at His coming	28 ...abide in Him (that...)

LIFE TOPIC 28

Hearing and Obeying

God's calling, purpose, and destiny for your life

Hearing and obeying God are two totally different things. When we don't want to obey God, we tend to hear the echoes of our own desires, and then claim we heard God. This is a dangerous thing, but can be avoided by remaining in fellowship with Jesus through the Holy Spirit, by acknowledging Him in all our ways throughout our days.

Luke 9:23, 24

23 If anyone desires to come after Me, let him deny himself, and take up his cross daily, and follow Me.

24 For whoever desires to save his life will lose it, but whoever loses his life for My sake will save it.

GOD'S CONDITIONAL PROMISES	RESPONSIBILITIES OF THE DOER OF THE WORD
3) Luke 9:23, 24	Luke 9:23, 24
23 If...	23 (If) anyone desires to come after Me ...let him deny himself ...and take up his cross daily ...and follow Me
24 For whoever... ...will save it	24 ...(whoever) loses his life for My sake (will...)

There are three Conditional Promises God makes to us.

There are five responsibilities that we must do for God.

28 LIFE TOPIC *Hearing and Obeying*

GOD'S CONDITIONAL PROMISES	RESPONSIBILITIES OF THE DOER OF THE WORD
3) Luke 9:23, 24	**Luke 9:23, 24**
23 If...	23 (If) anyone desires to come after Me ...let him deny himself ...and take up his cross daily ...and follow Me
24 For whoever...	24 ...(whoever) loses his life for My sake (will...)
...will save it	
5) Luke 17:20, 21, 33	**Luke 17:33**
20 The kingdom of God does not come with observation	
21 ...indeed, the kingdom of God is within you	
33 ...whoever...	33 ...(whoever) loses his life (will...)
...will preserve it	
6) John 14:12	**John 14:12**
12 ...he who...	12 ...(who) believes in Me (the...)
...the works that I do he will do also ...and greater works than these he will do, because I go to My Father	

GOD'S CONDITIONAL PROMISES	RESPONSIBILITIES OF THE DOER OF THE WORD
8) Rom. 12:2	**Rom. 12:1, 2**
	1 ...present your bodies a living sacrifice ...holy ...acceptable to God, which is your reasonable service 2 ...do not be conformed to this world ...but be transformed by the renewing of your mind (that...)
2 ...that you may prove what is that good ...and (prove what is that) acceptable ...and (prove what is that) perfect will of God	
14) Col. 4:17	**Col. 4:17**
	17 Take heed to the ministry which you have received in the Lord (that...)
17 ...that you may fulfill it	

GOD'S CONDITIONAL PROMISES	RESPONSIBILITIES OF THE DOER OF THE WORD
15) 1 Tim. 3:1	**1 Tim. 3:1, 2, 3, 4, 6, 7**
1 This is a faithful saying: If a man...	1 ...(man) desires the position of a bishop [overseer] (he...)
...he desires a good work	2 A bishop then must be blameless ...the husband of one wife ...temperate ...sober-minded ...of good behavior ...hospitable ...able to teach
	3 ...not given to wine ...not violent ...not greedy for money ...but gentle ...not quarrelsome ...not covetous [loving money and things]
	4 ...one who rules his own house well ...having his children in submission with all reverence
	6 ...not a novice [new convert]
	7 Moreover he must have a good testimony among those who are outside

GOD'S CONDITIONAL PROMISES	RESPONSIBILITIES OF THE DOER OF THE WORD
17) Heb. 5:4	Heb. 5:4
4 ...but he who is called by God, just as Aaron was	4 ...no man takes this honor to himself (but...)

LIFE TOPIC 29

Evil

Authority over demons and works of darkness

The same way you would take charge to rid your home of bugs, and deny entry into your home by thieves — don't allow sin, demons, and works of darkness to make their way into your life. Apply the full armor of God and stand, and live for who you are in Christ.

Mark 9:29

29 This kind can come out by nothing but prayer and fasting.

GOD'S CONDITIONAL PROMISES	RESPONSIBILITIES OF THE DOER OF THE WORD
1) Mark 9:29	Mark 9:29
29 This kind can come out by nothing but...	29 ...(but) prayer ...and fasting

There is one Conditional Promise God makes to us.

There are two responsibilities that we must do for God.

29 LIFE TOPIC   *Evil*

GOD'S CONDITIONAL PROMISES	RESPONSIBILITIES OF THE DOER OF THE WORD
1) Mark 9:29	**Mark 9:29**
29 This kind can come out by nothing but...	29 ...(but) prayer ...and fasting
2) Mark 9:39, 40	**Mark 9:39, 40**
39 ...for no one who... ...can soon afterward speak evil of Me 40 ...he who... ...is on our side	39 Do not forbid him ...(who) works a miracle in My name (can...) 40 ...(who) is not against us (is...)
3) Rom. 8:38, 39	**Rom. 8:38**
38 ...nor principalities ...nor powers... 39 ...shall be able to separate us from the love of God which is in Christ Jesus our Lord	38 ...I am persuaded

GOD'S CONDITIONAL PROMISES	RESPONSIBILITIES OF THE DOER OF THE WORD
4) 2 Cor. 10:3, 4, 6	**2 Cor. 10:3, 4, 5, 6**
	3 ...though we walk in the flesh (we...)
3 ...we do not war according to the flesh 4 For the weapons of our warfare are not carnal but mighty in God for...	4 ...(for) pulling down strongholds 5 ...casting down arguments ...and (casting down) every high thing that exalts itself against the knowledge of God ...bringing every thought into captivity to the obedience of Christ 6 ...and being ready to punish all disobedience (when...)
6 ...when your obedience is fulfilled	
6) James 4:7	**James 4:7**
	7 ...submit to God Resist the devil (and...)
7 ...and he will flee from you	

LIFE TOPIC 30

Being God's Friend

Pleasing and honoring Him

God plus you is the most powerful partnership you can have in this life. Being God's friend and knowing it, living it, and sharing it makes life worth living each and every day.

1 Samuel 2:30

30 ... for those who honor Me I will honor ...

GOD'S CONDITIONAL PROMISES	RESPONSIBILITIES OF THE DOER OF THE WORD
1) 1 Sam. 2:30	1 Sam. 2:30
30 ...for those who... ...I will honor	30 ...(who) honor Me (I...)

There are two Conditional Promises God makes to us.
There is one responsibility that we must do for God.

30 LIFE TOPIC *Being God's Friend*

GOD'S CONDITIONAL PROMISES	RESPONSIBILITIES OF THE DOER OF THE WORD
1) 1 Sam. 2:30	**1 Sam. 2:30**
30 ...for those who... ...I will honor	30 ...(who) honor Me (I...)
3) Ps. 33:5	**Ps. 33:5**
5 He loves...	5 ...(loves) righteousness ...and (He loves) justice
4) Ps. 50:23	**Ps. 50:23**
23 ...whoever ...glorifies Me	23 ...(whoever) offers praise (glorifies...)
6) Prov. 23:15, 16	**Prov. 23:15, 16**
15 ...if... ...My heart [the educator] will rejoice 16 ...yes, my inmost being will rejoice when...	15 ...(if) your heart [the pupil] is wise (My...) 16 ...(when) your lips speak right things
7) Matt. 5:8	**Matt. 5:8**
8 Blessed are... ...for they shall see God	8 ...(are) the pure [holy, separated to God] in heart (for...)

Being God's Friend   LIFE TOPIC 30

GOD'S CONDITIONAL PROMISES	RESPONSIBILITIES OF THE DOER OF THE WORD
8) Matt. 11:6	**Matt. 11:6**
6 …blessed is he who…	6 …(who) is not offended because of Me
9) John 8:31, 32	**John 8:31**
31 If… …you are My disciples indeed 32 And you shall know the truth …and the truth shall make you free	31 (If) you abide in My word (you…)
12) 2 Cor. 10:18	**2 Cor. 10:17**
18 For not he who commends himself is approved, but whom the Lord commends	17 …he who glories, let him glory in the Lord
13) Heb. 11:6	**Heb. 11:6**
6 …without… …it is impossible to please Him …for he who… …and that He is a rewarder of those who…	6 …(without) faith (it…) …(who) comes to God …must believe that He is (and…) …(who) diligently seek Him

30 LIFE TOPIC *Being God's Friend*

	GOD'S CONDITIONAL PROMISES	RESPONSIBILITIES OF THE DOER OF THE WORD
	14) Heb. 13:16	**Heb. 13:16**
	16 ...for with such sacrifices God is well pleased	16 ...do not forget to do good ...and to share (for...)
	16) 1 John 4:7, 11	**1 John 4:7, 11**
	7 ...for love is of God ...and everyone who... ...is born of God ...and knows God	7 ...let us love one another (for...) ...(who) loves (is...)
	11 ...Beloved, if...	11 ...(if) God so loved us, we also ought to love one another
	17) 3 John 11	**3 John 11**
	11 ...He who... ...is of God	11 ...do not imitate what is evil, but what is good ...(who) does good (is...)

GOD'S CONDITIONAL PROMISES	RESPONSIBILITIES OF THE DOER OF THE WORD
18.4) Ex. 19:5, 6	**Ex. 19:5**
5 ...if... ...then you shall be a special treasure to Me above all people 6 ...you shall be to Me a kingdom of priests ...and (you shall be to Me) a holy nation	5 ...(if) you will indeed obey My voice ...and keep My covenant (then...)

Symbolic Commentary
"But you are a chosen generation, a royal priesthood, a holy nation, His own special people, that you may proclaim the praises of Him who called you out of darkness into His marvelous light; who once were not a people but now are the people of God, who had not obtained mercy but now have obtained mercy" (1 Pet. 2:9-10). This calling by God is made complete in the New Testament believer. Hearing God's voice and keeping His covenant as a royal priest means the doer of the Word must live as a righteous worshiper of God. The calling from God as a holy nation means the doer of the Word is called to live a life of purity and holiness, and remains sanctified (set apart) from loving the things of the world more than God (see 1 John 2:15-17).

LIFE TOPIC 31

Spirit-filled Living

Working out your own salvation through spiritual gifts with power

God in you is more powerful than anything we can behold. Combine the knowledge that you are God's friend, with the reality that the Holy Spirit of God dwells in you and desires to work through you, and while no weapon formed against you can prosper — what you put your hand to can prosper. Therefore, walk in the Spirit of God and live.

43 Therefore I say to you, the kingdom of God will be taken from you and given to a nation bearing the fruits of it.

GOD'S CONDITIONAL PROMISES	RESPONSIBILITIES OF THE DOER OF THE WORD
1) Matt. 21:43	Matt. 21:43
43 ...the kingdom of God will be taken from you [who do not believe] and given to a nation [believer]	43 ...(nation) bearing the fruits of it

There is one Conditional Promise God makes to us.

There is one responsibility that we must do for God.

31 LIFE TOPIC   *Spirit-filled Living*

GOD'S CONDITIONAL PROMISES	RESPONSIBILITIES OF THE DOER OF THE WORD
1) Matt. 21:43	**Matt. 21:43**
43 ...the kingdom of God will be taken from you [who do not believe] and given to a nation [believer]	43 ...(nation) bearing the fruits of it
2) Acts 1:5, 8	**Acts 1:8**
5 ...for John truly baptized with water, but you shall be baptized with the Holy Spirit 8 ...you shall receive power when the Holy Spirit has come upon you ...and you shall...	8 ...(shall) be witnesses to Me in Jerusalem ...and in all Judea ...and Samaria ...and to the end of the earth

GOD'S CONDITIONAL PROMISES	RESPONSIBILITIES OF THE DOER OF THE WORD
3) Acts 2:38, 39	**Acts 2:38**
	38 ...repent and let every one of you be baptized in the name of Jesus Christ for the remission of sins (and...)
38 ...and you shall receive the gift of the Holy Spirit 39 For the promise is to you ...and (the promise is) to your children ...and (the promise is) to all who are afar off ...and (the promise is to) as many as the Lord our God will call	
5) Phil. 1:6	**Phil. 1:6**
	6 ...being confident of this very thing (that...)
6 ...that He who has begun a good work in you will complete it until the day of Jesus Christ	

LIFE TOPIC 32

Grace vs. Law

Being righteous in Christ, free from
sin and the curse of the law

God is a God of order and balance. He has established how to govern your life within the boundaries of authority. His Conditional Promises pave the
way for living confidently in His love, and among the
elders and leaders of the land. Because of the grace of
God, we can be faith-filled doers of the Word.

Romans 3:28; 4:5, 12, 16

28 Therefore we conclude that a man is justified by faith apart from the deeds of the law.

5 But to him who does not work but believes on Him who justifies the ungodly, his faith is accounted for righteousness,

12 ...but who also walk in the steps of the faith which our father Abraham had while still uncircumcised.

16 Therefore it is of faith that it might be according to grace, so that the promise might be sure to all the seed, not only to those who are of the law, but also to those who are of the faith of Abraham...

GOD'S CONDITIONAL PROMISES

RESPONSIBILITIES OF THE DOER OF THE WORD

1) Rom. 3:28; 4:5, 16	Rom. 3:28; 4:5, 12, 16
28 ...we conclude that a man is justified by... ...apart from the deeds of the law	28 ...(by) faith (apart...)
5 ...to him who...	5 ...(who) does not work ...but believes on Him who justifies the ungodly (his...)
...his faith is accounted for righteousness	12 ...(who) also walk in the steps of the faith which our father Abraham had while still uncircumcised
16 Therefore it is of faith that it might be according to grace, so that the promise might be sure to all the seed, not only to those who are of the law, but also to those who...	16 ...(who) are of the faith of Abraham

There are five Conditional Promises God makes to us.

There are five responsibilities that we must do for God.

32 LIFE TOPIC   *Grace vs. Law*

GOD'S CONDITIONAL PROMISES	RESPONSIBILITIES OF THE DOER OF THE WORD
1) Rom. 3:28; 4:5, 16	Rom. 3:28; 4:5, 12, 16
28 ...we conclude that a man is justified by... ...apart from the deeds of the law	28 ...(by) faith (apart...)
5 ...to him who... ...his faith is accounted for righteousness	5 ...(who) does not work ...but believes on Him who justifies the ungodly (his...) 12 ...(who) also walk in the steps of the faith which our father Abraham had while still uncircumcised
16 Therefore it is of faith that it might be according to grace, so that the promise might be sure to all the seed, not only to those who are of the law, but also to those who...	16 ...(who) are of the faith of Abraham

Grace vs. Law

LIFE TOPIC 32

GOD'S CONDITIONAL PROMISES	RESPONSIBILITIES OF THE DOER OF THE WORD
2) Rom. 5:17, 20, 21	Rom. 5:17
17 For if by the one man's offense death reigned through the one, much more those who...	
	17 ...(who) receive abundance of grace ...and (receive) of the gift of righteousness (will...)
...will reign in life through the One, Jesus Christ 20 Moreover the law entered that the offense might abound. But where sin abounded, grace abounded much more 21 so that as sin reigned in death, even so grace might reign through righteousness to eternal life through Jesus Christ our Lord	
6) Rom. 10:4	Rom. 10:4
4 ...Christ is the end of the law for righteousness to everyone who...	
	4 ...(who) believes

32 LIFE TOPIC *Grace vs. Law*

GOD'S CONDITIONAL PROMISES	RESPONSIBILITIES OF THE DOER OF THE WORD
7) Rom. 13:8, 10	Rom. 13:8, 9, 10

8   ...for he who...
    ...has fulfilled the law
	8 Owe no one anything
	    except to love one another
	    ...(who...) loves another (has...)
	9 ...You shall not
	    commit adultery
	    ...you shall not murder
	    ...you shall not steal
	    ...you shall not bear
	    false witness
	    ...you shall not covet
	    ...you shall love your
	    neighbor as yourself
	10 Love does no harm to a
	    neighbor (therefore...)

10 ...therefore love is the fulfillment of the law	
8) Gal. 3:11, 12, 13, 14	Gal. 3:11, 14

11 But that no one is justified
    [declared righteous] by
    the law in the sight of
    God is evident, for...
 	
12 ...the law is not of faith
13 Christ has redeemed us from
    the curse of the law, having
    become a curse for us
14 ...that the blessing of
    Abraham might come upon
    the Gentiles in Christ Jesus,
    that we might receive the
    promise of the Spirit...
	11 ...(for) the just shall
	    live by faith
	
	14 ...(Spirit) through faith

Grace vs. Law   **LIFE TOPIC 32**

GOD'S CONDITIONAL PROMISES	RESPONSIBILITIES OF THE DOER OF THE WORD
9) Gal. 3:24, 25	Gal. 3:24
24 …the law was our tutor [guardian responsible for the care and discipline of the children] to bring us to Christ, that we might be justified… 25 But after faith has come, we are no longer under a tutor	24 …(justified) by faith
11) Gal. 5:18, 19, 22, 23	Gal. 5:18, 22, 23
18 …if… …you are not under the law 19 Now the works of the flesh are evident 22 …the fruit of the Spirit is… 23 Against such there is no law	18 …(if) you are led by the Spirit (you…) 22 …(is) love …joy …peace …longsuffering …kindness …goodness …faithfulness 23 …gentleness …self-control

LIFE TOPIC 33

Spiritual Gifts

For service and ministry to others

What we can do ourselves falls within the limits of our natural abilities. However, when God intervenes through the Holy Spirit, what we do can be called supernatural. Our spiritual gifts make us more accountable to Jesus. As a Doer of the Word, we open the way for Him to work through us in the most meaningful and powerful ways.

Romans 10:17

17 So then faith comes by hearing,
and hearing by the word of God.

GOD'S CONDITIONAL PROMISES		**RESPONSIBILITIES OF THE DOER OF THE WORD**
1) Rom. 10:17		**Rom. 10:17**
17 So then faith comes by... ...and hearing by the word of God		17 ...(by) hearing (and...)

There are two Conditional Promises God makes to us.

There is one responsibility that we must do for God.

33 LIFE TOPIC *Spiritual Gifts*

GOD'S CONDITIONAL PROMISES	RESPONSIBILITIES OF THE DOER OF THE WORD
1) Rom. 10:17	**Rom. 10:17**
17 So then faith comes by... ...and hearing by the word of God	17 ...(by) hearing (and...)
4) 1 Cor. 12:3	**1 Cor. 12:3**
3 ...no one... ...calls Jesus accursed ...and no one can say that... ...except by the Holy Spirit	3 ...(one) speaking by the Spirit of God (calls...) ...(that) Jesus is Lord (except...)
6) 1 Cor. 14:33	**1 Cor. 14:26, 33, 40**
  33 ...God is not the author of confusion [disorder] ...but (God is the author) of peace, as in...	26 Let all things be done for edification 33 ...(in) all the churches of the saints 40 Let all things be done decently and in order

GOD'S CONDITIONAL PROMISES	RESPONSIBILITIES OF THE DOER OF THE WORD
7) Phil. 2:13	Phil. 2:12
13 ...for it is God who works in you both to will ...and to do for His good pleasure	12 ...work out your own salvation with fear [holy reverence] ...and trembling [humility]
11) 1 Pet. 4:11	1 Pet. 4:10, 11
11 ...that in all things God may be glorified through Jesus Christ ...to whom belong the glory ...and the dominion ...forever and ever	10 As each one has received a gift, minister it to one another ...as good stewards of the manifold grace of God 11 If anyone speaks, let him speak as the oracles of God If anyone ministers, let him do it as with the ability which God supplies (that...)

APPENDIX

A

Appendix A is a Topical Directory for locating God's Conditional Promises by Life Topics.

To search for God's Conditional Promises by Bible Books / Chapters / Verses, see Appendix B.

In this Appendix A, however, you will find the Conditional Promises located in the Unabridged Edition have been added, and are highlighted in gray for additional studies.

Since this book is the *Condensed Edition* of *The Conditional Promises of God,* not all of the Conditional Promises of God regarding His blessings are printed in their expanded form, as they are in the *Unabridged Edition.*

Note that Life Topics 1 and 14 are omitted from the Condensed Edition, and are found in their entirety in the Unabridged Edition.

— How to Use Appendix A —

2 LIFE TOPIC	*Family*

PAGE 30	Relationship to spouse, children, and future generations

GOD'S CONDITIONAL PROMISES	RESPONSIBILITIES OF THE DOER OF THE WORD
1) Deut. 4:40	Deut. 4:39, 40
2) Deut. 30:5, 6, 10	Deut. 30:2, 8, 10
3) Ps. 25:12, 13, 14	Ps. 25:12, 14
4) Ps. 103:17, 18	Ps. 103:18
5) Ps. 112:1, 2	Ps. 112:1, 2, 4, 5, 7
6) Ps. 127:5	Ps. 127:5
7) Ps. 128:3, 4, 6	Ps. 128:4

The Conditional Promises Topical Directory

LIFE TOPICS

1	**Environment**	Authority over the earth, elements, and living creatures
2	**Family**	Relationship to spouse, children, and future generations
3	**Offerings**	Of money, goods, time, and talents

15	**Persecution**	Finding hope, strength, and courage
16	**Death**	Never needing to fear it at any age
17	**Wisdom**	Instruction and direction for making decisions
18	**Children and Youth**	Temptation and adversity; sharing, overcoming, and encouraging others
19	**Eternal Life**	Assurance you are saved by Jesus Christ
20	**Fasting**	According to God's standards and directions
21	**Salvation**	Believing on Jesus Christ alone for eternal life
22	**Trials and Temptations**	Emerging the victor
23	**Repentance**	After giving in to temptation
24	**Prayer**	Asking, believing, and speaking by faith in Christ
25	**Preaching the Gospel**	Experiencing resistance, opposition, and the Holy Spirit's power
26	**Sins or Offenses**	Committed between believers

Reflection Notes

1 LIFE TOPIC *Enviroment*

PAGE 28	Authority over the earth, elements, and living creatures

GOD'S CONDITIONAL PROMISES	RESPONSIBILITIES OF THE DOER OF THE WORD
1) Gen. 1:26	Gen. 1:28
2) Ps. 37:9, 11	Ps. 37:7, 8, 9, 11
3) Ps. 67:6, 7	Ps. 67:5
4) Rom. 8:39	Rom. 8:38
5.4) Ps. 8:4, 5, 6, 7, 8	Ps. 8:3
6.4) Ps. 91:13	Ps. 91:2, 9

2 LIFE TOPIC *Family*

PAGE 30	Relationship to spouse, children, and future generations

GOD'S CONDITIONAL PROMISES	RESPONSIBILITIES OF THE DOER OF THE WORD
1) Deut. 4:40	Deut. 4:39, 40
2) Deut. 30:5, 6, 10	Deut. 30:2, 8, 10
3) Ps. 25:12, 13, 14	Ps. 25:12, 14
4) Ps. 103:17, 18	Ps. 103:18
5) Ps. 112:1, 2	Ps. 112:1, 2, 4, 5, 7
6) Ps. 127:5	Ps. 127:5
7) Ps. 128:3, 4, 6	Ps. 128:4
8) Ps. 145:4	Ps. 145:1, 2, 5, 6, 7
9) Prov. 20:7	Prov. 20:7
10) Prov. 22:6	Prov. 22:6

GOD'S CONDITIONAL PROMISES	RESPONSIBILITIES OF THE DOER OF THE WORD
11) Prov. 29:15, 17	Prov. 29:15, 17
12) Prov. 31:30	Prov. 31:30
13) Isa. 44:3, 4, 5	Isa. 44:2, 8
14) Isa. 59:20, 21	Isa. 59:20
15) Matt. 18:10, 14	Matt. 18:10
16) Matt. 19:5, 6	Matt. 19:5, 6
17) Matt. 19:14	Matt. 19:14
18) Mark 10:6, 8, 9	Mark 10:7, 9
19) 1 Cor. 7:14, 15	1 Cor. 7:10, 11, 15
20) Col. 3:21	Col. 3:21
21) 1 Pet. 3:1, 2, 4, 6	1 Pet. 3:1, 2, 3, 4, 6
22.4) Gen. 2:18, 24, 25	Gen. 2:23, 24
23.4) Gen. 17:7	Gen. 17:1, 9, 10
24.4) Gen. 22:16, 17, 18	Gen. 22:2, 3, 9, 10, 11, 12, 18
25.4) Josh. 14:9	Josh. 14:9
26.4) Ps. 102:12, 13, 16, 18, 28	Ps. 102:14, 15, 18
27.4) Isa. 54:3, 13	Isa. 54:1, 2, 4
28.4) Jer. 31:16, 17	Jer. 31:16
29.4) Eph. 5:26, 27, 28, 31	Eph. 5:25, 28, 31

3 LIFE TOPIC — *Offerings*

PAGE 34	Of money, goods, time, and talents

GOD'S CONDITIONAL PROMISES	RESPONSIBILITIES OF THE DOER OF THE WORD
1) Gen. 4:7	Gen. 4:7
2) Deut. 15:10	Deut. 15:7, 8, 9, 10, 11

GOD'S CONDITIONAL PROMISES	RESPONSIBILITIES OF THE DOER OF THE WORD
3) Ps. 112:1	Ps. 112:1, 9
4) Prov. 3:10	Prov. 3:9
5) Prov. 11:25	Prov. 11:25
6) Prov. 14:21	Prov. 14:21
7) Prov. 19:17	Prov. 19:17
8) Prov. 22:9	Prov. 22:9
9) Prov. 28:27	Prov. 28:27
10) Isa. 32:8	Isa. 32:8
11) Mal. 3:10, 11, 12	Mal. 3:10
12) Matt. 5:23, 25, 26	Matt. 5:23, 24, 25
13) Matt. 6:4	Matt. 6:1, 2, 3, 4
14) Matt. 6:21	Matt. 6:20
15) Mark 10:21	Mark 10:21
16) Mark 10:29, 30, 31	Mark 10:29, 31
17) Luke 6:38	Luke 6:38
18) Luke 11:41	Luke 11:41
19) Luke 14:14	Luke 14:13
20) Luke 18:29, 30	Luke 18:29, 30
21) Acts 20:32, 35	Acts 20:28, 32, 35
22) 2 Cor. 8:12, 14	2 Cor. 8:12
23) 2 Cor. 9:6, 7, 8	2 Cor. 9:6, 7
24) Gal. 6:7, 8, 9	Gal. 6:6, 7, 8, 9, 10
25) Phil. 4:18, 19	Phil. 4:14, 15, 16, 17, 18
26) 1 Tim. 5:17, 18	1 Tim. 5:17
27) Heb. 13:16	Heb. 13:16
28) 3 John 6, 8	3 John 5, 6, 8

GOD'S CONDITIONAL PROMISES	RESPONSIBILITIES OF THE DOER OF THE WORD
29.4) Eccl. 11:2	Eccl. 11:2
30.4) Isa. 32:17, 18, 20	Isa. 32:17, 20
31.4) Heb. 7:8	Heb. 7:8

.4) LIFE TOPIC   *Symbolic Conditional Promise:*
(Located at the end of each Life Topic)

PAGE 42	Using word pictures *(Located at the end of each chapter using .4 to identify it as symbolic)*

At the end of each life topic, the symbolic conditional promises which refer to that life topic are indicated by using a .4) after the regularly numbered conditional promise [i.e., 5.4) or 26.4).

5 LIFE TOPIC   *God, Man, and Society*

PAGE 44	Balanced relationship unity

GOD'S CONDITIONAL PROMISES	RESPONSIBILITIES OF THE DOER OF THE WORD
1) Gen. 15:1, 6	Gen. 15:1, 6
2) Gen. 17:2, 4, 6	Gen. 17:1
3) Ex. 20:6, 24	Ex. 20:3, 4, 5, 6, 7, 13, 14, 15, 16, 17, 23
4) Deut. 28:1, 2, 3	Deut. 28:1, 2
5) Deut. 28:9, 10	Deut. 28:9
6) 2 Sam. 22:26, 27, 28	2 Sam. 22:26, 27, 28
7) Ps. 4:3	Ps. 4:3
8) Ps. 15:1, 2, 3, 4, 5	Ps. 15:2, 3, 4, 5

GOD'S CONDITIONAL PROMISES	RESPONSIBILITIES OF THE DOER OF THE WORD
9) Ps. 18:25, 26, 27	Ps. 18:25, 26, 27
10) Ps. 19:7, 8, 9	Ps. 19:7, 10, 14
11) Ps. 33:12, 20, 21	Ps. 33:12, 20, 21
12) Ps. 34:8	Ps. 34:8, 9
13) Ps. 37:4, 5	Ps. 37:3, 4, 5
14) Ps. 40:4	Ps. 40:4
15) Ps. 40:17	Ps. 40:1, 8, 9, 10
16) Ps. 62:12	Ps. 62:1, 8, 10
17) Ps. 67:4	Ps. 67:3, 4
18) Ps. 73:1	Ps. 73:1
19) Ps. 84:4	Ps. 84:2, 4
20) Ps. 86:5	Ps. 86:5
21) Ps. 96:13	Ps. 96:1, 2, 3, 8, 9, 10
22) Ps. 98:9	Ps. 98:1, 4, 5, 6
23) Ps. 100:5	Ps. 100:1, 2, 3, 4
24) Ps. 103:6, 11, 13	Ps. 103:11, 13
25) Ps. 106:3	Ps. 106:3
26) Ps. 107:9, 43	Ps. 107:1, 2, 8, 9, 22, 32, 43
27) Ps. 112:1, 3, 4, 9	Ps. 112:1, 4, 5, 7
28) Ps. 117:2	Ps. 117:1
29) Ps. 118:26	Ps. 118:26
30) Ps. 119:74	Ps. 119:74
31) Ps. 119:101, 103, 104	Ps. 119:101, 102, 104
32) Ps. 119:171	Ps. 119:171, 172, 173, 174, 176
33) Ps. 128:1	Ps. 128:1
34) Ps. 146:5	Ps. 146:5

GOD'S CONDITIONAL PROMISES	RESPONSIBILITIES OF THE DOER OF THE WORD
35) Ps. 146:8	Ps.146:8
36) Ps. 147:11	Ps. 147:11
37) Prov. 2:9	Prov. 2:7
38) Prov. 2:21	Prov. 2:21
39) Prov. 3:4	Prov. 3:3
40) Prov. 3:22, 23, 24	Prov. 3:21
41) Prov. 3:33, 34, 35	Prov. 3:33, 34, 35
42) Prov. 8:32, 34, 35	Prov. 8:32, 33, 34, 35
43) Prov. 10:6, 7	Prov. 10:6
44) Prov. 11:9	Prov. 11:9
45) Prov. 11:18	Prov. 11:18
46) Prov. 11:27, 28, 30	Prov. 11:27, 28, 30
47) Prov. 12:2, 3, 7	Prov. 12:2, 3, 7
48) Prov. 12:19	Prov. 12:19
49) Prov. 12:22	Prov. 12:22
50) Prov. 13:13	Prov. 13:13
51) Prov. 13:18	Prov. 13:18
52) Prov. 14:19	Prov. 14:19
53) Prov. 15:8, 9	Prov. 15:8, 9
54) Prov. 15:21	Prov. 15:21
55) Prov. 15:26	Prov. 15:26
56) Prov. 15:29	Prov. 15:29
57) Prov. 16:7	Prov. 16:7
58) Prov. 16:20	Prov. 16:20
59) Prov. 18:16	Prov. 18:16
60) Prov. 18:18	Prov. 18:18

61) Prov. 18:22	Prov. 18:22
62) Prov. 19:11	Prov. 19:11
63) Prov. 19:23	Prov. 19:23
64) Prov. 21:3	Prov. 21:3
65) Prov. 22:4	Prov. 22:4
66) Prov. 22:11	Prov. 22:11
67) Prov. 24:25	Prov. 24:23, 25
68) Prov. 25:15	Prov. 25:15
69) Prov. 29:18	Prov. 29:18
70) Prov. 30:5	Prov. 30:5
71) Eccl. 8:5	Eccl. 8:5
72) Isa. 30:18	Isa. 30:18
73) Isa. 33:6	Isa. 33:6
74) Isa. 49:23	Isa. 49:23
75) Isa. 57:1	Isa. 57:1
76) Isa. 64:4, 5	Isa. 64:4, 5
77) Isa. 66:2	Isa. 66:2
78) Jer. 17:10	Jer. 17:10
79) Jer. 18:7, 8	Jer. 18:8, 11
80) Ezek. 18:4, 5, 6, 7, 8, 9	Ezek. 18:5, 6, 7, 8, 9
81) Dan. 9:4	Dan. 9:4
82) Amos 5:14	Amos 5:14, 15
83) Mic. 2:7	Mic. 2:7
84) Hab. 3:19	Hab. 3:18
85) Zeph. 3:19	Zeph. 3:14, 16
86) Hag. 2:4, 5	Hag. 2:4, 5
87) Zech. 3:7	Zech. 3:7

GOD'S CONDITIONAL PROMISES	RESPONSIBILITIES OF THE DOER OF THE WORD
88) Mal. 1:9	Mal. 1:9
89) Matt. 5:7	Matt. 5:7
90) Matt. 5:9	Matt. 5:9
91) Matt. 5:16	Matt. 5:16
92) Matt. 5:45	Matt. 5:44, 48
93) Matt. 6:14	Matt. 6:14
94) Matt. 7:1, 5	Matt. 7:1, 5
95) Matt. 7:12	Matt. 7:12
96) Mark 3:35	Mark 3:35
97) Mark 9:49	Mark 9:50
98) Luke 6:27, 35, 37, 38	Luke 6:27, 28, 29, 30, 31, 35, 36, 37, 38
99) Luke 10:27, 28	Luke 10:27
100) Luke 14:11	Luke 14:11
101) Luke 18:22	Luke 18:20, 22
102) Luke 20:18	Luke 20:18
103) John 4:23, 24	John 4:23, 24
104) John 9:31	John 9:31
105) John 12:25, 26	John 12:25, 26
106) John 12:44, 45, 46	John 12:44, 45, 46
107) John 13:20	John 13:20
108) John 14:15, 16, 17, 18, 19, 20, 21, 23	John 14:15, 21, 23
109) John 15:8	John 15:8
110) John 15:16, 17	John 15:16, 17
111) Acts 2:47	Acts 2:46, 47
112) Rom. 1:6, 7	Rom. 1:5
113) Rom. 2:1	Rom. 2:1

GOD'S CONDITIONAL PROMISES	RESPONSIBILITIES OF THE DOER OF THE WORD
114) Rom. 12:19, 20	Rom. 12:18, 19, 20, 21
115) Rom. 13:3	Rom. 13:1, 3, 5
116) Rom. 13:8, 9, 10	Rom. 13:8, 9, 10
117) Rom. 15:7	Rom. 15:7
118) 1 Cor. 1:27, 28, 29, 30, 31	1 Cor. 1:29, 31
119) 1 Cor. 3:21, 23	1 Cor. 3:21
120) 1 Cor. 12:31; 13:8, 13	1 Cor. 13:4, 5, 6, 7; 14:1
121) 2 Cor. 2:14, 15, 16	2 Cor. 2:14, 17
122) Eph. 5:16	Eph. 5:15, 16, 17, 18, 19, 20, 21
123) Eph. 6:8	Eph. 6:5, 6, 7, 8
124) Phil. 2:15	Phil. 2:14, 16
125) Phil. 4:5	Phil. 4:4, 5
126) Col. 2:8, 9, 10	Col. 2:8
127) Col. 3:4, 10, 11	Col. 3:5, 8, 9, 10
128) Col. 3:24	Col. 3:22, 23, 24
129) 1 Thess. 2:4	1 Thess. 2:4
130) 1 Thess. 5:18, 24	1 Thess. 5:13, 15
131) 1 Tim. 2:2	1 Tim. 2:1, 2
132) 1 Tim. 6:1	1 Tim. 6:1
133) 1 Tim. 6:1, 2	1 Tim. 6:2
134) 2 Tim. 2:19	2 Tim. 2:19
135) Heb. 11:14, 16	Heb. 11:13, 14, 16
136) Heb. 12:14, 15, 16	Heb. 12:14, 15
137) Heb. 13:17	Heb. 13:17
138) James 1:18, 20, 21, 25	James 1:16, 19, 21, 25
139) James 2:5, 8	James 2:5, 8
140) 1 Pet. 1:13, 17, 18, 19, 20, 21	1 Pet. 1:13, 14, 15, 16, 17, 18, 21

GOD'S CONDITIONAL PROMISES	RESPONSIBILITIES OF THE DOER OF THE WORD
141.4) Gen. 12:2, 3	Gen. 12:1
142.4) Deut. 11:16, 26, 27	Deut. 11:1, 8, 16, 27, 32
143.4) 1 Kgs. 6:12, 13; 9:3, 4	1 Kgs. 6:12; 9:4
144.4) Ps. 11:5, 7	Ps. 11:1, 5, 7
145.4) Ps. 41:10, 11, 12	Ps. 41:4, 10
146.4) Ps. 65:4	Ps. 65:4
147.4) Ps. 75:10	Ps. 75:1, 9, 10
148.4) Ps. 81:8, 10	Ps. 81:8, 9, 10
149.4) Ps. 89:15, 16, 17	Ps. 89:15, 16
150.4) Prov. 1:33	Prov. 1:33
151.4) Isa. 57:13	Isa. 57:13
152.4) Isa. 61:1, 5, 6, 7	Isa. 61:1, 2, 3, 6
153.4) Jer. 7:3, 5, 6, 7, 23	Jer. 7:3, 5, 6, 23
154.4) Matt. 5:3	Matt. 5:3
155.4) Matt. 5:6	Matt. 5:6
156.4) Luke 12:1, 2, 3	Luke 12:1
157.4) 1 Cor. 7:22	1 Cor. 7:17, 20, 23, 24
158.4) 2 Pet. 1:2, 3, 4	2 Pet. 1:2, 3, 4

6 LIFE TOPIC   *Physical Health*

PAGE 54	Eating, drinking, exercise, and rest

GOD'S CONDITIONAL PROMISES	RESPONSIBILITIES OF THE DOER OF THE WORD
1) Ex. 15:26	Ex. 15:26
2) Ex. 20:6, 12, 24	Ex. 20:6, 12
3) Deut. 4:40	Deut. 4:39, 40

GOD'S CONDITIONAL PROMISES	RESPONSIBILITIES OF THE DOER OF THE WORD
4) Deut. 28:1, 2, 4	Deut. 28:1, 2
5) Deut. 28:9, 11	Deut. 28:9
6) Ps. 34:12	Ps. 34:13, 14
7) Ps. 36:9	Ps. 36:7
8) Ps. 41:1, 2, 3	Ps. 41:1
9) Ps. 91:16	Ps. 91:2, 9
10) Ps. 92:12, 13, 14, 15	Ps. 92:12, 13
11) Ps. 103:3, 4, 5	Ps. 103:1, 2
12) Ps. 103:17	Ps. 103:17, 18
13) Ps. 145:19, 20	Ps. 145:19, 20, 21
14) Ps. 146:8	Ps. 146:2
15) Prov. 3:2	Prov. 3:1
16) Prov. 3:8	Prov. 3:7
17) Prov. 4:10	Prov. 4:10
18) Prov. 4:22	Prov. 4:20, 21, 22
19) Prov. 9:11, 12	Prov. 9:12
20) Prov. 10:3	Prov. 10:3
21) Prov. 10:27, 28, 29	Prov. 10:27, 28, 29
22) Prov. 13:3	Prov. 13:3
23) Prov. 15:4	Prov. 15:4
24) Prov. 15:13, 15	Prov. 15:13, 15
25) Prov. 16:24	Prov. 16:24
26) Prov. 17:22	Prov. 17:22
27) Prov. 18:14	Prov. 18:14
28) Prov. 18:21	Prov. 18:21
29) Prov. 28:14	Prov. 28:14

30) Eccl. 5:12	Eccl. 5:12
31) Eccl. 7:12	Eccl. 7:12
32) Eccl. 8:1	Eccl. 8:1
33) Jer. 30:17	Jer. 30:9, 10
34) Zeph. 3:19	Zeph. 3:14, 16
35) Matt. 6:22	Matt. 6:22
36) Matt. 11:28, 29, 30	Matt. 11:28, 29
37) Luke 11:34, 36	Luke 11:35, 36
38) Acts 11:9	Acts 11:9
39) Rom. 8:6	Rom. 8:6
40) Col. 2:21, 22, 23	Col. 2:16, 18; 3:1, 2
41) 1 Thess. 5:18, 24	1 Thess. 5:16, 18
42) 1 Tim. 2:15	1 Tim. 2:15
43) 1 Tim. 4:4	1 Tim. 4:4
44) 1 Tim. 4:8	1 Tim. 4:8
45) Titus 1:15	Titus 1:15
46) 1 Pet. 5:14	1 Pet. 5:14
47.4) Deut. 11:8, 9, 16	Deut. 11:8, 16
48.4) Ps. 138:8	Ps. 138:1, 2
49.4) Prov. 14:30	Prov. 14:30
50.4) Prov. 22:5	Prov. 22:5
51.4) Jer. 17:24, 25, 26	Jer. 17:21, 22, 24
52.4) Luke 8:48, 50	Luke 8:48, 50, 52
53.4) Acts 10:15	Acts 10:15
54.4) Acts 14:10	Acts 14:9

7 LIFE TOPIC — *Leadership and Authority*

PAGE 62	Personal, business, or ministry work

GOD'S CONDITIONAL PROMISES	RESPONSIBILITIES OF THE DOER OF THE WORD
1) Deut. 28:1, 2, 6	Deut. 28:1, 2
2) Deut. 28:13	Deut. 28:13, 14
3) 2 Chron. 15:2, 7	2 Chron. 15:2, 7
4) Ps. 25:3, 9, 10	Ps. 25:1, 2, 3, 5, 9, 10
5) Ps. 37:4, 5	Ps. 37:3, 4, 5
6) Ps. 115:13	Ps. 115:13
7) Ps. 119:32	Ps. 119:27, 30, 31, 32, 33, 34, 35
8) Ps. 119:105	Ps. 119:106
9) Ps. 119:165	Ps. 119:165, 166, 167, 168
10) Ps. 127:1	Ps. 127:1
11) Ps. 127:1	Ps. 127:1
12) Ps. 147:6	Ps. 147:6
13) Prov. 4:12, 13	Prov. 4:13
14) Prov. 10:30, 31, 32	Prov. 10:30, 31, 32
15) Prov. 11:3	Prov. 11:3
16) Prov. 12:24	Prov. 12:24
17) Prov. 14:14	Prov. 14:14
18) Prov. 15:19	Prov. 15:19
19) Prov. 16:3	Prov. 16:3
20) Prov. 16:13	Prov. 16:13
21) Prov. 28:20	Prov. 28:20
22) Prov. 29:2, 6, 14	Prov. 29:2, 6, 14
23) Prov. 29:23	Prov. 29:23

GOD'S CONDITIONAL PROMISES	RESPONSIBILITIES OF THE DOER OF THE WORD
24) Eccl. 7:8	Eccl. 7:8
25) Ezek. 33:9	Ezek. 33:9
26) Matt. 23:12	Matt. 23:8, 9, 10, 12
27) Mark 10:42, 43, 44, 45	Mark 10:43
28) Luke 6:40	Luke 6:40
29) Luke 9:48	Luke 9:48
30) Luke 22:26, 28, 29, 30	Luke 22:26, 28
31) Acts 20:32, 35	Acts 20:28, 32, 35
32) 1 Cor. 4:2	1 Cor. 4:2
33) 1 Cor. 9:14, 17	1 Cor. 9:14, 17
34) 2 Cor. 6:3	2 Cor. 6:3, 4, 5, 6, 7, 8, 9, 10
35) Eph. 4:4, 5, 6	Eph. 4:1, 2, 3
36) Eph. 4:7, 12, 15, 16	Eph. 4:11, 14, 15
37) Eph. 6:9	Eph. 6:9
38) Col. 4:1	Col. 4:1
39) 1 Tim. 1:18	1 Tim. 1:19
40) 1 Tim. 3:13	1 Tim. 3:8, 9, 10, 11, 12, 13
41) 1 Tim. 4:6, 8	1 Tim. 4:6, 7, 8, 10
42) 1 Tim. 5:4	1 Tim. 5:1, 2, 3
43) 1 Tim. 5:17, 18	1 Tim. 5:17
44) Titus 1:6, 9	Titus 1:6, 7, 8, 9
45) Titus 3:14	Titus 3:14
46) James 3:1	James 3:1
47.4) Ex. 18:19, 23	Ex. 18:19, 20, 21, 23
48.4) Deut. 11:8, 13, 14, 16	Deut. 11:8, 13, 16
49.4) Deut. 28:1	Deut. 28:1

GOD'S CONDITIONAL PROMISES	RESPONSIBILITIES OF THE DOER OF THE WORD
50.4) 1 Sam. 24:19, 20; 26:25	1 Sam. 24:6
51.4) Ps. 2:8, 12	Ps. 2:8, 10, 11, 12
52.4) Ps. 18:28, 29, 30	Ps. 18:30
53.4) Prov. 8:17	Prov. 8:17
54.4) Jer. 15:19, 20, 21	Jer. 15:19
55.4) Jer. 22:4	Jer. 22:3
56.4) Matt. 26:52	Matt. 26:52
57.4) John 10:2	John 10:2, 4
58.4) John 13:10, 14, 15, 17	John 13:10, 14, 15, 17

8 LIFE TOPIC — *Stewardship*

PAGE 66	Managing money, material things, and time

GOD'S CONDITIONAL PROMISES | RESPONSIBILITIES OF THE DOER OF THE WORD

GOD'S CONDITIONAL PROMISES	RESPONSIBILITIES OF THE DOER OF THE WORD
1) Deut. 4:40	Deut. 4:39, 40
2) Deut. 28:1, 8	Deut. 28:1
3) Deut. 30:5, 10	Deut. 30:2, 8, 10
4) Josh. 1:5, 7, 8, 9	Josh. 1:6, 7, 8, 9
5) Ps. 1:1, 3	Ps. 1:1, 2
6) Ps. 15:5	Ps. 15:5
7) Ps. 25:12, 13, 14	Ps. 25:12, 14
8) Ps. 33:18, 19	Ps. 33:18
9) Ps. 34:9, 10	Ps. 34:9, 10
10) Ps. 36:8	Ps. 36:7
11) Ps. 37:4, 5	Ps. 37:3, 4, 5

GOD'S CONDITIONAL PROMISES	RESPONSIBILITIES OF THE DOER OF THE WORD
12) Ps. 37:17, 19, 29, 31	Ps. 37:17, 21, 27, 31
13) Ps. 84:11, 12	Ps. 84:2, 4, 5, 11, 12
14) Ps. 85:8, 9, 12, 13	Ps. 85:8, 9
15) Ps. 91:9, 10	Ps. 91:2, 9
16) Ps. 112:1, 3	Ps. 112:1, 4, 5, 7
17) Ps. 119:72	Ps. 119:67, 69, 70
18) Ps. 128:2	Ps. 128:2
19) Prov. 8:9, 11	Prov. 8:9, 10
20) Prov. 10:4, 5	Prov. 10:4, 5
21) Prov. 11:15	Prov. 11:15
22) Prov. 12:11, 12	Prov. 12:11, 12
23) Prov. 12:14	Prov. 12:14
24) Prov. 13:2	Prov. 13:2
25) Prov. 13:4	Prov. 13:4
26) Prov. 13:11	Prov. 13:11
27) Prov. 14:11	Prov. 14:11
28) Prov. 14:23	Prov. 14:23
29) Prov. 15:6	Prov. 15:6
30) Prov. 18:20	Prov. 18:20
31) Prov. 20:13	Prov. 20:13
32) Prov. 21:5	Prov. 21:5
33) Prov. 22:4	Prov. 22:4
34) Prov. 24:3, 4	Prov. 24:3, 4
35) Prov. 28:25	Prov. 28:25
36) Isa. 1:19	Isa. 1:19
37) Jer. 11:4, 5	Jer. 11:4, 6, 7

God's Conditional Promises	Responsibilities of the Doer of the Word
38) Matt. 6:32, 33, 34	Matt. 6:25, 31, 33, 34
39) Matt. 19:29	Matt. 19:29
40) Mark 10:23, 24, 27	Mark 10:23, 24, 27
41) Luke 12:15, 30, 31, 32, 33	Luke 12:15, 22, 24, 27, 29, 31, 32, 33
42) Luke 16:10	Luke 16:10
43) Luke 18:29, 30	Luke 18:29
44) Phil. 4:13	Phil. 4:11, 12
45) 1 Thess. 4:9, 10, 12	1 Thess. 4:9, 11
46) 1 Tim. 5:17, 18	1 Tim. 5:17
47) 1 Tim. 6:6	1 Tim. 6:6, 8, 11, 12
48) 1 Tim. 6:17, 18, 19	1 Tim. 6:17, 18
49.4) Gen. 22:16, 17, 18	Gen. 22:2, 3, 9, 10, 11, 12, 18
50.4) Deut. 15:4, 5, 6	Deut. 15:1, 2, 3, 5, 6
51.4) Deut. 28:1, 2, 4, 5	Deut. 28:1, 2
52.4) Deut. 28:9, 11, 12	Deut. 28:9, 12
53.4) 2 Chron. 7:14	2 Chron. 7:14
54.4) Ps. 23:1	Ps. 23: 1, 4
55.4) Prov. 8:20, 21	Prov. 8:21
56.4) Prov. 27:26, 27	Prov. 27:23, 25
57.4) Prov. 28:19	Prov. 28:19
58.4) Eccl. 11:1	Eccl. 11:1
59.4) Isa. 30:19, 23	Isa. 30:19, 22
60.4) Isa. 57:13	Isa. 57:13
61.4) Mic. 4:13	Mic. 4:13
62.4) Matt. 5:5	Matt. 5:5
63.4) Matt. 25:21, 23, 29	Matt. 25:21, 23

GOD'S CONDITIONAL PROMISES	RESPONSIBILITIES OF THE DOER OF THE WORD
64.4) Rom. 13:5, 6	Rom. 13:5, 6, 7
65.4) Heb. 7:8	Heb. 7:8

9 LIFE TOPIC   *Backsliding*

PAGE 74   Returning to God from living in sin

GOD'S CONDITIONAL PROMISES	RESPONSIBILITIES OF THE DOER OF THE WORD
1) Deut. 30:5, 10	Deut. 30:2, 8, 10
2) Ps. 34:15, 17, 18	Ps. 34:15, 17, 18
3) Ps. 51:17	Ps. 51:3, 17
4) Ps. 145:14, 15	Ps. 145:10, 11, 12, 15
5) Prov. 3:12	Prov. 3:11
6) Prov. 16:6	Prov. 16:6
7) Isa. 1:18	Isa. 1:16, 17, 18
8) Isa. 29:24; 30:15	Isa. 29:23, 24; 30:15
9) Isa. 44:21, 22	Isa. 44:22
10) Isa. 46:13	Isa. 46:9, 12
11) Isa. 55:7	Isa. 55:6, 7
12) Isa. 57:15, 18, 19	Isa. 57:15
13) Jer. 3:12, 14, 15, 22; 4:1	Jer. 3:12, 13, 14, 19, 22; 4:1
14) Jer. 24:6, 7	Jer. 24:7
15) Jer. 29:11, 12, 13, 14	Jer. 29:12, 13
16) Jer. 35:15	Jer. 35:15
17) Ezek. 11:17, 19, 20	Ezek. 11:18
18) Ezek. 18:21, 22, 27, 28	Ezek. 18:21, 22, 27, 28, 31

GOD'S CONDITIONAL PROMISES	RESPONSIBILITIES OF THE DOER OF THE WORD
19) Ezek. 33:14, 15, 16, 19	Ezek. 33:14, 15, 19
20) Zeph. 3:13, 20	Zeph. 3:13, 14, 16
21) Zech. 1:3	Zech. 1:3, 4
22) Mal. 3:6, 7	Mal. 3:7
23) Luke 15:7, 10	Luke 15:7, 10
24) Heb. 12:6, 7, 9, 11	Heb. 12:5, 7, 9, 11
25) James 5:19, 20	James 5:20
26.4) Ps. 116:15	Ps. 116:15
27.4) Ps. 126:5, 6	Ps. 126:5, 6
28.4) Isa. 30:19, 20, 21	Isa. 30:19, 22
29.4) Isa. 31:5	Isa. 31:6, 7
30.4) Isa. 52:12	Isa. 52:11
31.4) Isa. 65:8, 13, 14, 16	Isa. 65:16, 18
32.4) Ezek. 37:21, 22, 23, 26, 27	Ezek. 37:23, 24
33.4) Hos. 14:4, 5, 6, 7, 9	Hos. 14:1, 2, 9
34.4) Joel 2:13, 18, 19, 23, 25, 26, 27	Joel 2:12, 13, 15, 16, 17, 21, 23
35.4) Mic. 2:12, 13	Mic. 2:12, 13
36.4) Eph. 5:13, 14	Eph. 5:14

10 LIFE TOPIC   *Older Generation*

PAGE 80	Mature, seasoned adulthood

GOD'S CONDITIONAL PROMISES	RESPONSIBILITIES OF THE DOER OF THE WORD
1) Ps. 115:13	Ps. 115:13
2) Prov. 12:28	Prov. 12:28
3) Prov. 16:31	Prov. 16:31

GOD'S CONDITIONAL PROMISES	RESPONSIBILITIES OF THE DOER OF THE WORD
4) Prov. 20:29	Prov. 20:29
5) Prov. 22:4	Prov. 22:4
6) Prov. 28:16	Prov. 28:16
7) Eccl. 7:12	Eccl. 7:12
8) Isa. 46:4	Isa. 46:3
9) Eph. 6:1, 3	Eph. 6:2

11 LIFE TOPIC *Confrontation*

PAGE 84	Relationship or circumstantial barriers

GOD'S CONDITIONAL PROMISES	RESPONSIBILITIES OF THE DOER OF THE WORD
1) Deut. 28:1, 7	Deut. 28:1
2) Deut. 30:7, 10	Deut. 30:2, 8, 10
3) 2 Chron. 16:9	2 Chron. 16:9
4) 2 Chron. 20:9, 15, 17, 20	2 Chron. 20:3, 4, 9, 12, 15, 17, 18, 19, 20, 21
5) Ps. 3:3, 5, 7, 8	Ps. 3:4, 5, 6
6) Ps. 5:4, 5, 6, 11, 12	Ps. 5:7, 11, 12
7) Ps. 7:8, 9, 10, 11	Ps. 7:10, 17
8) Ps. 9:9, 10, 12, 13	Ps. 9:1, 2, 10, 11, 12, 14
9) Ps. 17:6, 7; 18:1, 2, 3	Ps. 17:3, 4, 6, 7; 18:1, 2, 3, 6
10) Ps.18:32, 33, 34, 47, 48, 50	Ps. 18:49
11) Ps. 20:6	Ps. 20:7, 8
12) Ps. 25:2	Ps. 25:1, 2, 5
13) Ps. 37:39, 40	Ps. 37:39, 40
14) Ps. 42:8	Ps. 42:11

GOD'S CONDITIONAL PROMISES	RESPONSIBILITIES OF THE DOER OF THE WORD
15) Ps. 46:1, 7	Ps. 46:2
16) Ps. 55:16, 17, 22	Ps. 55:16, 17, 22, 23
17) Ps. 57:2, 3	Ps. 57:1, 2, 6, 7, 9
18) Ps. 59:9, 10, 11, 17	Ps. 59:9, 16, 17
19) Ps. 71:3, 5, 7, 20, 21, 23, 24	Ps. 71:1, 8, 14, 15, 16, 22, 23, 24
20) Ps. 91:1, 9, 10, 11, 12, 14, 15	Ps. 91:1, 2, 9, 14, 15
21) Ps. 92:4	Ps. 92:1, 2, 3
22) Ps. 97:10, 11	Ps. 97:10, 11, 12
23) Ps. 108:13	Ps. 108:1, 3
24) Ps. 119:98	Ps. 119:97, 99, 100
25) Ps. 138:6, 7	Ps. 138:1, 2
26) Prov. 2:7, 8	Prov. 2:7
27) Prov. 3:26	Prov. 3:25
28) Prov. 12:13	Prov. 12:13
29) Prov. 21:23	Prov. 21:23
30) Prov. 29:25	Prov. 29:25
31) Isa. 41:12, 13	Isa. 41:13, 16
32) Isa. 59:1, 19, 20	Isa. 59:20
33) Mic. 7:7, 8, 9, 18, 19	Mic. 6:8; 7:5, 7, 9
34) Nah. 1:7	Nah. 1:7
35) Zeph. 3:19	Zeph. 3:14, 16
36) Mark 9:23	Mark 9:23
37) Luke 12:5, 6, 7	Luke 12:4, 5, 7
38) Rom. 8:28	Rom. 8:28
39) 2 Cor. 4:10, 11, 14, 15, 16, 17, 18	2 Cor. 4:8, 9, 10, 14, 15, 16, 18

GOD'S CONDITIONAL PROMISES	RESPONSIBILITIES OF THE DOER OF THE WORD
40) 2 Thess. 1:5, 6, 7, 8	2 Thess. 1:4
41) 1 Pet. 5:10	1 Pet. 5:10
42) 1 John 4:18	1 John 4:18
43) Rev. 21:7	Rev. 21:7
44.4) 2 Sam. 22:2, 3, 4, 18, 19, 20, 48, 49	2 Sam. 22:3, 4, 7, 22, 23, 24, 38, 39, 50
45.4) Ps. 25:15	Ps. 25:15
46.4) Ps. 125:1, 2	Ps. 125:1
47.4) Isa. 28:16	Isa. 28:16
48.4) Isa. 33:15, 16	Isa. 33:15
49.4) Isa. 54:17	Isa. 54:1, 2, 4

12 LIFE TOPIC *Anxiety, Depression, and Oppression*

PAGE 90	God's provision for overcoming

GOD'S CONDITIONAL PROMISES	RESPONSIBILITIES OF THE DOER OF THE WORD
1) Ps. 4:1	Ps. 4:1
2) Ps. 4:7, 8	Ps. 4:4, 5, 8
3) Ps. 10:14, 17, 18	Ps. 10:14, 17
4) Ps. 16:5, 6, 7, 8, 9, 10, 11	Ps. 16:1, 7, 8
5) Ps. 29:11	Ps. 29:1, 2
6) Ps. 30:5	Ps. 30:1, 4, 12
7) Ps. 31:3, 4, 15, 19, 20, 23, 24	Ps. 31:1, 5, 19, 23, 24
8) Ps. 37:4, 5	Ps. 37:3, 4, 5
9) Ps. 43:2, 5	Ps. 43:4, 5

GOD'S CONDITIONAL PROMISES	RESPONSIBILITIES OF THE DOER OF THE WORD
10) Ps. 50:15	Ps. 50:15
11) Ps. 56:8, 9	Ps. 56:3, 4, 10, 11, 12
12) Ps. 73:23, 24, 26, 28	Ps. 73:25, 28
13) Ps. 84:5, 6, 7, 11, 12	Ps. 84:2, 4, 5, 11, 12
14) Ps. 94:12, 13, 14, 15, 18, 19	Ps. 94:12, 15
15) Ps. 119:1, 2	Ps. 119:1, 2, 3, 4, 7, 8, 15, 16, 24
16) Ps. 119:114	Ps. 119:114, 115
17) Ps. 127:2	Ps. 127:2
18) Ps. 139:10	Ps. 139:14
19) Ps. 144:15	Ps. 144:9, 15
20) Ps. 145:18	Ps. 145:18
21) Ps. 145:19, 20	Ps. 145:19, 20, 21
22) Ps. 146:8	Ps. 146:2, 8
23) Ps. 147:3	Ps. 147:1
24) Prov. 11:4, 5, 6, 8	Prov. 11:4, 5, 6, 8
25) Prov. 12:6	Prov. 12:6
26) Prov. 12:20, 21	Prov. 12:20, 21
27) Prov. 13:21	Prov. 13:21
28) Prov. 18:10	Prov. 18:10
29) Isa. 26:3, 4	Isa. 26:3, 4
30) Isa. 40:31	Isa. 40:31
31) Isa. 41:10	Isa. 41:10
32) Isa. 52:6	Isa. 52:1, 2
33) Isa. 57:1, 2	Isa. 57:1
34) Isa. 60:1, 2, 3	Isa. 60:1, 4
35) Luke 6:21	Luke 6:21

GOD'S CONDITIONAL PROMISES	RESPONSIBILITIES OF THE DOER OF THE WORD
36) Luke 8:8, 10, 15	Luke 8:8, 15
37) John 16:33	John 16:33
38) Rom. 5:1, 2, 3, 4, 5	Rom. 5:1, 2, 3, 4
39) Rom. 8:28	Rom. 8:28
40) Rom. 15:13; 16:20	Rom. 15:13; 16:16, 17, 19
41) 2 Cor. 12:9, 10	2 Cor. 12:9, 10
42) Gal. 6:15, 16	Gal. 6:15, 16
43) Eph. 6:23, 24	Eph. 6:24
44) Phil. 4:9	Phil. 4:8, 9
45) 1 Thess. 5:18, 24	1 Thess. 5:14
46) Heb. 6:11	Heb. 6:11
47) James 4:8, 10	James 4:8, 9, 10
48) 1 Pet. 1:6, 7, 9	1 Pet. 1:6, 7, 8, 9
49) 1 Pet. 3:10	1 Pet. 3:10, 11
50) 1 Pet. 5:7	1 Pet. 5:7
51) 1 Pet. 5:10	1 Pet. 5:10
52) 1 John 4:18	1 John 4:18
53) 2 John 2, 3	2 John 2
54.4) Ps. 23:1, 2, 3, 4, 6	Ps. 23:1, 4
55.4) Ps. 27:1, 5, 6, 14	Ps. 27:3, 6, 14
56.4) Ps. 118:6, 14	Ps. 118:6, 8, 9
57.4) Ps. 121:2, 3, 5, 7, 8	Ps. 121:1
58.4) Isa. 43:1, 2	Isa. 43:1
59.4) Isa. 54:14	Isa. 54:1, 2, 4
60.4) Jer. 42:10, 11	Jer. 42:10, 11, 19

13 LIFE TOPIC *The Poor*

PAGE 98   Homeless, abandoned, widowed, and parentless

GOD'S CONDITIONAL PROMISES	RESPONSIBILITIES OF THE DOER OF THE WORD
1) Ps. 9:18	Ps. 9:18
2) Ps. 10:14, 17, 18	Ps. 10:14, 17
3) Ps. 12:5; 14:6	Ps. 13:5, 6
4) Ps. 68:5, 6	Ps. 68:4
5) Ps. 69:32, 33	Ps. 69:30, 32
6) Ps. 102:17	Ps. 102:17
7) Ps. 107:41, 43	Ps. 107: 42, 43
8) Ps. 113:7, 8, 9	Ps. 113:1, 3
9) Ps. 116:6	Ps. 116:6, 9, 13, 14, 17
10) Ps. 140:12	Ps. 140:6, 13
11) Ps. 145:14, 15, 16	Ps. 145:10, 11, 12, 15
12) Ps. 145:19, 20	Ps. 145:19, 20, 21
13) Ps. 146:5, 7, 9	Ps. 146:2, 5
14) Prov. 13:6	Prov. 13:6
15) Prov. 15:25	Prov. 15:25
16) Rom. 8:28	Rom. 8:28
17) 2 Cor. 6:16, 17, 18	2 Cor. 6:14, 17; 7:1
18) 1 Tim. 5:16	1 Tim. 5:16
19) James 1:27	James 1:27
20) 1 Pet. 5:10	1 Pet. 5:10
21) 1 John 4:18	1 John 4:18
22.4) Isa. 54:3, 4, 5, 8, 10	Isa. 54:1, 2, 4
23.4) Luke 6:20, 21	Luke 6:20, 21

14 LIFE TOPIC   *Angels*

PAGE 102	Our authority and their assistance

GOD'S CONDITIONAL PROMISES	RESPONSIBILITIES OF THE DOER OF THE WORD
1) Ps. 34:7	Ps. 34:7
2) Rom. 8:38, 39	Rom. 8:38, 39

15 LIFE TOPIC   *Persecution*

PAGE 104	Finding hope, strength, and courage

GOD'S CONDITIONAL PROMISES	RESPONSIBILITIES OF THE DOER OF THE WORD
1) Ps. 34:19, 20, 22	Ps. 34:19, 22
2) Ps. 37:4, 5, 6	Ps. 37:3, 4, 5
3) Ps. 37:32, 33, 34	Ps. 37:32, 34
4) Ps. 64:10	Ps. 64:10
5) Ps. 109:31	Ps. 109:30
6) Ps. 115:11	Ps. 115:11
7) Ps. 115:13	Ps. 115:13
8) Ps.119:86	Ps. 119:81, 83
9) Ps. 146:5, 7	Ps. 146:2, 5
10) Prov. 25:21, 22	Prov. 25:21
11) Prov. 28:10	Prov. 28:10
12) Prov. 28:18	Prov. 28:18
13) Prov. 28:26	Prov. 28:26
14) Eccl. 8:12	Eccl. 8:12
15) Isa. 41:11	Isa. 41:13, 16

16) Isa. 51:8	Isa. 51:7
17) Jer. 17:7, 8	Jer. 17:7
18) Jer. 31:3, 4, 8, 9, 13, 14	Jer. 31:7, 10, 14
19) Lam. 3:22, 23, 25, 31, 32, 33	Lam. 3:24, 25, 26, 28, 40, 41, 55
20) Zech. 9:11, 12, 15, 16, 17; 10:1, 3, 5, 6, 7, 8, 12	Zech. 10:1, 7, 9, 12
21) Zech. 13:8, 9	Zech. 13:9
22) Matt. 5:10, 11	Matt. 5:10, 12
23) Matt. 10:39	Matt. 10:39
24) Matt. 16:25	Matt. 16:25
25) Matt. 19:30; 20:16	Matt. 19:30; 20:16
26) Luke 6:22, 23	Luke 6:23
27) Luke 12:11, 12	Luke 12:11
28) Luke 14:26, 27	Luke 14:26, 27
29) Luke 21:34, 36	Luke 21:34, 36
30) John 15:18, 19, 20; 16:1, 4	John 15:18
31) John 16:33	John 16:33
32) Rom. 8:16, 17, 18	Rom. 8:17, 18
33) Rom. 8:28	Rom. 8:28
34) Rom. 8:38, 39	Rom. 8:38
35) 1 Cor. 16:22	1 Cor. 16:13, 14, 22
36) 2 Cor. 1:3, 4, 7	2 Cor. 1:4, 7
37) Phil. 1:28, 29	Phil. 1:27, 28
38) 2 Tim. 1:14	2 Tim. 1:13, 14
39) 2 Tim. 3:12	2 Tim. 3:12
40) Titus 2:8	Titus 2:1, 7, 8
41) Heb. 12:3	Heb. 12:3

GOD'S CONDITIONAL PROMISES	RESPONSIBILITIES OF THE DOER OF THE WORD
42) James 1:3, 4	James 1:2, 3, 4
43) James 5:11	James 5:11
44) 1 Pet. 2:19, 20, 21	1 Pet. 2:18, 19, 20, 21
45) 1 Pet. 4:14, 16, 17, 19	1 Pet. 4:14, 15, 16, 17, 19
46) 1 Pet. 5:10	1 Pet. 5:10
47) 1 John 4:18	1 John 4:18
48) Rev. 14:12	Rev. 14:12
49.4) Gen. 7:1, 9, 10, 16	Gen. 7:1, 5, 7
50.4) Isa. 35:4, 10	Isa. 35:3, 4
51.4) Isa. 54:15	Isa. 54:1, 2, 4
52.4) Jer. 23: 3, 4, 8	Jer. 23:7, 8
53.4) Rev. 16:15	Rev. 16:15

16 LIFE TOPIC   *Death*

PAGE 112	Never needing to fear it at any age

GOD'S CONDITIONAL PROMISES	RESPONSIBILITIES OF THE DOER OF THE WORD
1) Ps. 37:18	Ps. 37:18
2) Ps. 49:15	Ps. 49:5
3) Ps. 116:15	Ps. 116:15
4) Ps. 118:20	Ps. 118:20
5) John 5:28, 29	John 5:28
6) John 8:51	John 8:51
7) Rom. 8:38, 39	Rom. 8:38
8) 1 Cor. 6:14, 17	1 Cor. 6:17

GOD'S CONDITIONAL PROMISES	RESPONSIBILITIES OF THE DOER OF THE WORD
9) 1 Cor. 15:58	1 Cor. 15:58
10) 2 Cor. 1:9, 10	2 Cor. 1:10
11) Phil. 1:19, 20, 21	Phil. 1:19, 20, 25
12) 1 Thess. 4:14, 15, 17	1 Thess. 4:14, 18
13) 1 John 4:18	1 John 4:18
14) Rev. 2:10, 11	Rev. 2:10, 11
15) Rev. 14:13	Rev. 14:13
16.4) Ps. 48:14	Ps. 48:9

17 LIFE TOPIC — *Wisdom*

PAGE 116	Instruction and direction for making decisions

GOD'S CONDITIONAL PROMISES	RESPONSIBILITIES OF THE DOER OF THE WORD
1) Job 28:28	Job 28:28
2) Ps. 36:9	Ps. 36:7
3) Ps. 37:30	Ps. 37:30
4) Ps. 111:10	Ps. 111:1, 10
5) Prov. 1:2, 3, 4, 5, 6, 7	Prov. 1:7
6) Prov. 2:1, 5, 7	Prov. 2:1, 2, 3, 4, 7
7) Prov. 3:6	Prov. 3:5, 6
8) Prov. 3:13, 18	Prov. 3:13, 18
9) Prov. 4:6, 8, 9	Prov. 4:1, 2, 4, 5, 6, 7, 8
10) Prov. 8:9	Prov. 8:9
11) Prov. 9:10	Prov. 9:10
12) Prov. 11:2	Prov. 11:2
13) Prov. 11:14	Prov. 11:14

GOD'S CONDITIONAL PROMISES	RESPONSIBILITIES OF THE DOER OF THE WORD
14) Prov. 12:8	Prov. 12:8
15) Prov. 13:10	Prov. 13:10
16) Prov. 13:15	Prov. 13:15
17) Prov. 14:6	Prov. 14:6
18) Prov. 14:18	Prov. 14:18
19) Prov. 15:23	Prov. 15:23
20) Prov. 15:31, 32, 33	Prov. 15:31, 32, 33
21) Prov. 16:21, 22, 23	Prov. 16:21, 22, 23
22) Prov. 17:20	Prov. 17:20
23) Prov. 17:24	Prov. 17:24
24) Prov. 19:8	Prov. 19:8
25) Prov. 20:15	Prov. 20:15
26) Prov. 21:11	Prov. 21:11
27) Prov. 22:18, 19	Prov. 22:17, 18
28) Prov. 25:11, 12	Prov. 25:11, 12
29) Prov. 28:2, 5	Prov. 28:2, 5
30) Eccl. 2:26	Eccl. 2:26
31) Eccl. 7:12	Eccl. 7:12
32) Eccl. 7:19	Eccl. 7:19
33) Eccl. 10:10, 12	Eccl. 10:10, 12
34) Jer. 33:3	Jer. 33:3
35) Matt. 7:7, 8	Matt. 7:7, 8
36) Matt. 7:24	Matt. 7:24
37) Matt. 12:35, 37	Matt. 12:35, 37
38) Matt. 13:12	Matt. 13:12
39) Mark 4:9, 11, 20	Mark 4:9, 20

40) Mark 4:24, 25	Mark 4:24, 25
41) Luke 6:47, 48	Luke 6:47, 48
42) Luke 10:23	Luke 10:23
43) John 7:17	John 7:17
44) John 8:47	John 8:47
45) John 14:26, 27	John 14:27
46) 1 Cor. 1:27, 28, 29, 30, 31	1 Cor. 1:29, 31
47) 1 Cor. 2:9	1 Cor. 2:9
48) 1 Cor. 2:14, 15, 16	1 Cor. 2:14, 15
49) 1 Cor. 3:18	1 Cor. 3:18
50) 1 Cor. 8:1	1 Cor. 8:1
51) 1 Cor. 10:6, 11, 12	1 Cor. 10:6, 7, 8, 9, 10, 12
52) Eph. 1:17, 18, 19	Eph. 1:19
53) Col. 1:9, 10, 11	Col. 1:4, 8, 12
54) Col. 2:2	Col. 2:6, 7
55) 2 Tim. 2:7	2 Tim. 2:7
56) 2 Tim. 3:15	2 Tim. 3:15
57) James 1:5	James 1:5, 6
58) James 3:17, 18	James 3:13, 17, 18
59) 1 Pet. 2:2, 3	1 Pet. 2:1, 2, 3
60) 2 Pet. 1:8, 10	2 Pet. 1:5, 6, 7, 8, 10
61) Rev. 1:3	Rev. 1:3
62.4) John 11:9	John 11:9
63.4) Acts 5:38, 39	Acts 5:35, 38
64.4) 1 John 2:27	1 John 2:27

18 LIFE TOPIC   *Children and Youth*

PAGE 124	Temptation and adversity; sharing, overcoming, and encouraging others

GOD'S CONDITIONAL PROMISES	RESPONSIBILITIES OF THE DOER OF THE WORD
1) Ex. 20:6, 12, 24	Ex. 20:6, 12
2) Ps. 115:13	Ps. 115:13
3) Prov. 1:2, 3, 4, 5, 6, 7	Prov. 1:7
4) Prov. 2:11, 12, 13, 14, 15, 16, 17, 20	Prov. 2:10, 11
5) Prov. 5:2	Prov. 5:1
6) Prov. 6:22	Prov. 6:20, 21
7) Prov. 14:22	Prov. 14:22
8) Prov. 14:26	Prov. 14:26
9) Prov. 15:5	Prov. 15:5
10) Prov. 16:17	Prov. 16:17
11) Prov. 16:32	Prov. 16:32
12) Prov. 19:20	Prov. 19:20
13) Prov. 20:11	Prov. 20:11
14) Prov. 20:29	Prov. 20:29
15) Prov. 29:16	Prov. 29:16
16) Eccl. 7:12	Eccl. 7:12
17) Eccl. 7:18	Eccl. 7:16, 17, 18
18) Eccl. 11:9	Eccl. 11:9, 10
19) Jer. 1:8	Jer. 1:7, 8
20) Ezek. 18:14, 17, 19, 20	Ezek. 18:14, 15, 16, 17, 19, 20
21) Matt. 23:12	Matt. 23:12
22) Mark 7:15, 16	Mark 7:14, 16

GOD'S CONDITIONAL PROMISES	RESPONSIBILITIES OF THE DOER OF THE WORD
23) Luke 11:28	Luke 11:28
24) Luke 18:14, 16, 17	Luke 18:14, 16, 17
25) John 15:8	John 15:8
26) Rom. 8:28	Rom. 8:28
27) Eph. 6:1, 3	Eph. 6:1, 2
28) Col. 3:20	Col. 3:20
29) 1 Thess. 5:18, 24	1 Thess. 5:14
30) 1 Tim. 4:15, 16	1 Tim. 4:12, 13, 14, 15, 16
31) Heb. 13:17	Heb. 13:17
32) 1 Pet. 5:5	1 Pet. 5:5
33) 1 John 4:18	1 John 4:18
34.4) Prov. 1:9	Prov. 1:8
35.4) Eccl. 7:26	Eccl. 7:26
36.4) Matt. 7:16, 20	Matt. 7:15

19 LIFE TOPIC *Eternal Life*

PAGE 130	Assurance you are saved by Jesus Christ

GOD'S CONDITIONAL PROMISES	RESPONSIBILITIES OF THE DOER OF THE WORD
1) Ps. 32:1, 2	Ps. 32:2
2) Ps. 149:4	Ps. 149:4
3) Prov. 10:2	Prov. 10:2
4) Prov. 19:16	Prov. 19:16
5) Prov. 23:18	Prov. 23:17
6) Isa. 45:22, 25	Isa. 45:22, 25
7) Isa. 56:2, 5	Isa. 56:1

GOD'S CONDITIONAL PROMISES	RESPONSIBILITIES OF THE DOER OF THE WORD
8) Jer. 30:8, 10, 11	Jer. 30:9, 10
9) Joel 2:28, 29, 32	Joel 2:32
10) Nah. 1:7	Nah. 1:7
11) Zech. 2:10	Zech. 2:10
12) Zech. 8:3, 7, 8, 12, 13	Zech. 8:9, 13, 15, 16, 17, 19
13) Mal. 4:2, 3	Mal. 4:2, 3, 4
14) Matt. 5:19	Matt. 5:19
15) Matt. 13:43	Matt. 13:43
16) Mark 2:27	Mark 2:27
17) Mark 9:41	Mark 9:41
18) Luke 8:21	Luke 8:21
19) John 6:35, 37, 40	John 6:35, 37, 40
20) John 10:27, 28, 29	John 10:27
21) Acts 13:38, 39	Acts 13:39
22) Rom. 1:16, 17	Rom. 1:16, 17
23) Rom. 2:28, 29	Rom. 2:29
24) Rom. 4:22, 23, 24	Rom. 4:20, 21, 24
25) Rom. 5:10, 11	Rom. 5:11
26) Rom. 8:14, 16	Rom. 8:14, 15
27) Rom. 15:4, 6	Rom. 15:1, 2, 5
28) 1 Cor. 1:2, 3	1 Cor. 1:2
29) 2 Cor. 1:20, 21, 22	2 Cor. 1:24
30) 2 Cor. 3:14, 16, 17, 18	2 Cor. 3:16
31) 2 Cor. 5:1, 3, 4, 5	2 Cor. 5:1, 2, 3, 4, 6, 7, 8
32) 2 Cor. 5:14, 15, 17	2 Cor. 5:14, 15, 16, 17
33) 2 Cor. 13:5	2 Cor. 13:5
34) Gal. 2:16, 20, 21	Gal. 2:16, 20, 21

GOD'S CONDITIONAL PROMISES	RESPONSIBILITIES OF THE DOER OF THE WORD
35) Gal. 3:6, 7, 8, 9	Gal. 3:6, 7, 9
36) Gal. 3:26, 27, 28, 29	Gal. 3:26, 27, 29
37) Eph. 1:3, 4, 5, 6, 7, 8, 9, 10, 11, 12, 13, 14	Eph. 1:12, 13
38) Eph. 4:21, 24	Eph. 4:21, 22, 23, 24
39) Phil. 3:3	Phil. 3:1, 2, 3
40) Col. 1:12, 21, 22, 23	Col. 1:23
41) 1 Thess. 1:4, 10	1 Thess. 1:3, 4
42) 1 Thess. 5:2, 4, 5, 9, 10	1 Thess. 5:2, 6, 8, 11
43) 2 Thess. 2:13, 14	2 Thess. 2:13, 15
44) 2 Tim. 2:11, 12, 13	2 Tim. 2:11, 12, 13
45) Titus 2:11, 14	Titus 2:12, 13, 14
46) Heb. 3:6	Heb. 3:6
47) Heb. 3:14, 15	Heb. 3:14, 15
48) Heb. 6:11, 12, 14, 18	Heb. 6:11, 12, 15, 18
49) Heb. 10:34, 35, 36, 38, 39	Heb. 10:34, 35, 36, 38, 39
50) Heb. 12:2	Heb. 12:1, 2
51) 1 Pet. 1:3, 4, 5	1 Pet. 1:5
52) 1 Pet. 2:5, 6, 9	1 Pet. 2:6, 9
53) 1 Pet. 2:24, 25	1 Pet. 2:24, 25
54) 1 John 1:7	1 John 1:7
55) 1 John 2:3, 5, 6	1 John 2:3, 5, 6
56) 1 John 2:17, 23, 24, 25	1 John 2:17, 23, 24
57) 1 John 2:29	1 John 2:29
58) 1 John 3:3, 6, 7, 9	1 John 3:3, 6, 7, 9
59) 1 John 4:12, 15, 16	1 John 4:12, 15, 16
60) 1 John 5:18	1 John 5:18, 21
61) 2 John 9	2 John 9

GOD'S CONDITIONAL PROMISES	RESPONSIBILITIES OF THE DOER OF THE WORD
62) Rev. 3:5, 6	Rev. 3:2, 3, 5, 6
63.4) Ps. 69:35, 36	Ps. 69:36
64.4) Isa. 8:14	Isa. 8:13, 17
65.4) Isa. 40:10, 11	Isa. 40:9
66.4) Isa. 51:3, 4	Isa. 51:1, 2, 4
67.4) Isa. 62:1, 2, 3, 12	Isa. 62:10, 11
68.4) John 15:1, 2, 3, 4, 5	John 15:2, 4, 5
69.4) Rom. 11:18, 22, 23	Rom. 11:18, 20, 22, 23
70.4) 1 Pet. 3:21, 22	1 Pet. 3:21
71.4) 2 Pet. 1:8, 10, 11	2 Pet. 1:5, 6, 7, 8, 10

20 LIFE TOPIC *Fasting*

PAGE 136	According to God's standards and directions

GOD'S CONDITIONAL PROMISES	RESPONSIBILITIES OF THE DOER OF THE WORD
1) Isa. 58:8, 9	Isa. 58:6, 7
2) Matt. 6:17, 18	Matt. 6:17, 18
3.4) Matt. 9:15	Matt. 9:15
4.4) Luke 5:35	Luke 5:35

21 LIFE TOPIC *Salvation*

PAGE 140	Believing on Jesus Christ alone for eternal life

GOD'S CONDITIONAL PROMISES	RESPONSIBILITIES OF THE DOER OF THE WORD
1) Ps. 91:16	Ps. 91:2, 9
2) Ps. 146:8	Ps.146:2

GOD'S CONDITIONAL PROMISES	RESPONSIBILITIES OF THE DOER OF THE WORD
3) Jer. 12:16	Jer. 12:16
4) Zeph. 3:9, 11, 12, 13, 15, 17	Zeph. 3:9, 10, 11, 12, 13, 14, 16
5) Matt. 4:19	Matt. 4:19
6) Matt. 5:23, 25, 26	Matt. 5:23, 24, 25
7) Matt. 10:40	Matt. 10:40
8) Matt. 18:3, 4, 5	Matt. 18:3, 4, 5
9) Matt. 19:17, 21	Matt. 19:17, 18, 19, 21
10) Matt. 19:29	Matt. 19:29
11) Mark 1:15, 17	Mark 1:15, 17
12) Mark 2:17	Mark 2:17
13) Mark 8:34, 35	Mark 8:34, 35
14) Mark 9:37	Mark 9:37
15) Mark 10:14, 15	Mark 10:15
16) Mark 10:29, 30, 31	Mark 10:29, 31
17) Luke 7:23	Luke 7:23
18) Luke 12:8	Luke 12:8
19) Luke 15:7, 10	Luke 15:7
20) Luke 20:18	Luke 20:18
21) John 1:12, 13	John 1:12, 13
22) John 3:3, 5, 15, 16, 18, 21, 36	John 3:3, 5, 7, 15, 16, 18, 21, 36
23) John 5:24	John 5:24
24) John 6:47	John 6:47
25) John 7:37, 38	John 7:37, 38
26) John 8:12	John 8:12
27) John 8:47	John 8:47
28) John 11:25, 26	John 11:25, 26

GOD'S CONDITIONAL PROMISES	RESPONSIBILITIES OF THE DOER OF THE WORD
29) John 14:6, 7, 9	John 14:7, 9, 11
30) John 20:29	John 20:29
31) Acts 2:21	Acts 2:21
32) Acts 3:19, 20, 21	Acts 3:19
33) Acts 4:10, 12	Acts 4:12
34) Acts 10:34, 35	Acts 10:35
35) Acts 16:31	Acts 16:31
36) Rom. 3:22, 26, 28	Rom. 3:22, 26, 28
37) Rom. 8:28	Rom. 8:28
38) Rom. 10:4, 8, 9, 10, 11, 12, 13	Rom. 10:4, 9, 10, 11, 12, 13
39) 1 Cor. 1:18, 21	1 Cor. 1:18, 21
40) 2 Cor. 7:10	2 Cor. 7:10
41) Gal. 3:22	Gal. 3:22
42) Eph. 2:8, 9, 10	Eph. 2:8, 10
43) Phil. 3:8, 9	Phil. 3:7, 8, 9
44) 1 Thess. 2:12	1 Thess. 2:12
45) 1 Tim. 4:10	1 Tim. 4:10
46) Titus 3:7, 8	Titus 3:8
47) Heb. 4:1, 3, 7, 10, 11	Heb. 4:1, 3, 7, 10, 11
48) Heb. 7:25	Heb. 7:25
49) Heb. 9:15	Heb. 9:15
50) 1 Pet. 3:9	1 Pet. 3:8, 9
51) 2 Pet. 3:9	2 Pet. 3:9
52) 1 John 5:4, 5, 10, 12	1 John 5:4, 5, 10, 12
53) Rev. 2:7	Rev. 2:2, 3, 4, 5, 6, 7
54) Rev. 3:18, 19, 20, 21, 22	Rev. 3:18, 19, 20, 21, 22

GOD'S CONDITIONAL PROMISES	RESPONSIBILITIES OF THE DOER OF THE WORD
55) Rev. 21:6	Rev. 21:6
56.4) Ex. 12:13, 43	Ex. 12:43, 48
57.4) Ps. 130:7, 8	Ps. 130:1, 5, 6
58.4) Mic. 4:1	Mic. 4:1, 2
59.4) Luke 13:30	Luke 13:24
60.4) John 4:14	John 4:14
61.4) John 6:51, 53, 54, 56, 57	John 6:51, 53, 54, 56, 57
62.4) John 10:9	John 10:9
63.4) John 15:1, 2, 3, 4, 5	John 15:2, 4, 5
64.4) Eph. 5:13, 14	Eph. 5:14

22 LIFE TOPIC *Trials and Temptations*

PAGE 148	Emerging the victor

GOD'S CONDITIONAL PROMISES	RESPONSIBILITIES OF THE DOER OF THE WORD
1) Prov. 14:27	Prov. 14:27
2) Prov. 15:27	Prov. 15:27
3) Isa. 57:1	Isa. 57:1
4) Matt. 26:41	Matt. 26:41
5) Mark 4:22, 23	Mark 4:23, 24
6) Rom. 13:11, 12	Rom. 13:11, 12, 13, 14
7) 1 Cor. 6:19, 20	1 Cor. 6:20
8) 1 Cor. 9:27	1 Cor. 9:26, 27
9) 1 Cor. 15:33, 34	1 Cor. 15:33, 34
10) Gal. 5:16, 24, 25	Gal. 5:16, 24, 25, 26
11) 1 Thess. 4:1, 3, 7	1 Thess. 4:1, 2

GOD'S CONDITIONAL PROMISES	RESPONSIBILITIES OF THE DOER OF THE WORD
12) 1 Thess. 5:18, 24	1 Thess. 5:19, 20, 21, 22
13) Heb. 2:1	Heb. 2:1
14) Heb. 3:12, 13	Heb. 3:12, 13
15) James 1:12	James 1:12
16) James 1:27	James 1:27
17) 1 Pet. 4:1, 2	1 Pet. 4:1, 2, 6
18) 1 Pet. 5:8, 9	1 Pet. 5:8, 9
19) 2 Pet. 2:9	2 Pet. 2:9
20) 2 Pet. 3:17	2 Pet. 3:14, 15, 17, 18
21) 1 John 5:18	1 John 5:18, 21
22) 3 John 11	3 John 11
23) Rev. 12:11; 13:9, 10	Rev. 12:11, 12, 17; 13:9, 10
24.4) Ps. 125:3, 4	Ps. 125:3, 4
25.4) Matt. 18:8, 9	Matt. 18:8, 9
26.4) Luke 22:40, 46	Luke 22:40, 46
27.4) 1 Cor. 3:16, 17	1 Cor. 3:17
28.4) 1 Cor. 5:6, 7	1 Cor. 5:7, 8
29.4) 1 Cor. 10:13	1 Cor. 10:14
30.4) Heb. 5:14	Heb. 5:14

23 LIFE TOPIC — *Repentance*

PAGE 152	After giving in to temptation

GOD'S CONDITIONAL PROMISES	RESPONSIBILITIES OF THE DOER OF THE WORD
1) Ps. 32:7, 8, 10	Ps. 32:5, 10, 11
2) Prov. 28:13	Prov. 28:13
3) Isa. 43:25, 26	Isa. 43:26

GOD'S CONDITIONAL PROMISES	RESPONSIBILITIES OF THE DOER OF THE WORD
4) Ezek. 16:59, 60, 61, 62, 63	Ezek. 16:61, 63
5) Matt. 4:17	Matt. 4:17
6) Luke 8:17, 18	Luke 8:18
7) Luke 15:7, 10	Luke 15:7, 10
8) Rom. 2:2, 4, 6, 7, 10, 11	Rom. 2:7, 10
9) Heb. 4:16	Heb. 4:16
10) James 4:17	James 4:17
11) 1 John 1:9	1 John 1:9
12.4) Matt. 5:4	Matt. 5:4
13.4) Luke 13:3, 5	Luke 13:3, 5
14.4) Rev. 2:17	Rev. 2:16, 17

24 LIFE TOPIC — *Prayer*

PAGE 156	Asking, believing, and speaking by faith in Christ

GOD'S CONDITIONAL PROMISES	RESPONSIBILITIES OF THE DOER OF THE WORD
1) Ps. 28:8	Ps. 28:1, 7
2) Matt. 6:6	Matt. 6:6, 7
3) Matt. 15:28	Matt. 15:28
4) Matt. 16:19	Matt. 16:19
5) Matt. 17:20	Matt. 17:20
6) Matt. 18:18, 19, 20	Matt. 18:18, 19, 20
7) Matt. 21:21, 22	Matt. 21:21, 22
8) Mark 11:23, 24, 25	Mark 11:22, 23, 24, 25
9) Luke 11:9, 10, 13	Luke 11:9, 10, 13
10) Luke 18:7, 8	Luke 18:7

GOD'S CONDITIONAL PROMISES	RESPONSIBILITIES OF THE DOER OF THE WORD
11) John 15:7	John 15:7
12) John 20:21, 23	John 20:22, 23
13) Phil. 4:7	Phil. 4:6
14) 1 Thess. 5:18, 24	1 Thess. 5:17
15) James 5:14, 15, 16	James 5:14, 15, 16
16) 1 Pet. 3:7	1 Pet. 3:7
17) 1 Pet. 3:12	1 Pet. 3:12
18) 1 John 3:22	1 John 3:22, 23
19) 1 John 5:14, 15	1 John 5:14, 15
20.4) Luke 17:6	Luke 17:6
21.4) John 14:13, 14	John 14:13, 14
22.4) John 16:23, 24, 25, 26, 27	John 16:23, 24, 26, 27

25 LIFE TOPIC   *Preaching the Gospel*

PAGE 166	Experiencing resistance, opposition, and the Holy Spirit's power

GOD'S CONDITIONAL PROMISES	RESPONSIBILITIES OF THE DOER OF THE WORD
1) Ezek. 3:17, 19, 21	Ezek. 3:19, 21
2) Matt. 9:37	Matt. 9:38
3) Matt. 28:20	Matt. 28:19, 20
4) Mark 16:16, 17, 18	Mark 16:15, 16, 17
5) Luke 5:10	Luke 5:10
6) Luke 10:7, 11, 16	Luke 10:2, 3, 9
7) John 12:32, 36	John 12:32, 35, 36
8) Acts 5:32	Acts 5:32
9) Rom. 10:15	Rom. 10:15

GOD'S CONDITIONAL PROMISES	RESPONSIBILITIES OF THE DOER OF THE WORD
10) 1 Cor. 9:19, 20, 21, 22, 23	1 Cor. 9:19, 20, 21, 22, 23
11) 1 Cor. 10:23, 26, 28, 29, 33	1 Cor. 10:24, 25, 27, 28, 31, 32, 33; 11:1
12) 2 Cor. 4:6, 7	2 Cor. 4:2, 5
13) 2 Cor. 6:1, 2	2 Cor. 6:1, 2
14) Eph. 3:6, 9, 10, 11, 12	Eph. 3:2, 9, 10, 12
15) Col. 4:6	Col. 4:2, 5, 6
16) 2 Tim. 1:7, 9, 12	2 Tim. 1:8, 12
17) 2 Tim. 2:9, 10	2 Tim. 2:10
18) 2 Tim. 2:25, 26	2 Tim. 2:23, 24, 25
19) Philem. 6	Philem. 5, 6
20) 1 Pet. 3:13, 14, 16	1 Pet. 3:13, 14, 15, 16
21) 1 John 1:3, 4	1 John 1:2
22) 1 John 4:2, 4, 6	1 John 4:2, 6
23) 1 John 4:18	1 John 4:18
24.4) Gen. 17:2, 4, 6	Gen. 17:1
25.4) John 4:35, 36, 37	John 4:35, 36
26.4) Acts 18:10	Acts 18:9
27.4) Acts 26:16, 17, 18	Acts 26:16, 18
28.4) Eph. 5:13, 14	Eph. 5:14
29.4) 1 Thess. 2:4, 19, 20	1 Thess. 2:4

26 LIFE TOPIC   *Sins or Offenses*

PAGE 172	Committed between believers

GOD'S CONDITIONAL PROMISES	RESPONSIBILITIES OF THE DOER OF THE WORD
1) Matt. 5:23, 25, 26	Matt. 5:23, 24, 25

GOD'S CONDITIONAL PROMISES	RESPONSIBILITIES OF THE DOER OF THE WORD
2) Matt. 18:15, 16, 17	Matt. 18:15, 16, 17
3) Matt. 18:35	Matt. 18:35
4) Luke 6:42	Luke 6:42
5) Luke 9:50	Luke 9:50
6) Luke 17:1, 3, 4	Luke 17:3, 4
7) John 13:34, 35	John 13:34, 35
8) Rom. 14:3, 4, 12, 14, 17, 18, 20, 22, 23	Rom. 14:1, 3, 13, 14, 16, 18, 19, 20, 21, 22
9) Rom. 15:7	Rom. 15:7
10) 1 Cor. 1:9	1 Cor. 1:10
11) 1 Cor. 4:20	1 Cor. 4:6
12) 1 Cor. 5:5	1 Cor. 5:4, 5
13) 1 Cor. 5:13	1 Cor. 5:11, 13
14) 1 Cor. 12:24, 26, 27	1 Cor. 12:25, 26
15) 2 Cor. 2:11	2 Cor. 2:4, 5, 7, 8, 9, 10, 11
16) 2 Cor. 13:11	2 Cor. 13:11, 12
17) Gal. 5:8, 9, 14	Gal. 5:10, 13, 14
18) Gal. 6:2, 3, 4	Gal. 6:2, 4, 5
19) Col. 3:12, 14, 15	Col. 3:12, 13, 14, 15, 16, 17
20) 1 Thess. 4:6	1 Thess. 4:3, 4, 5, 6
21) 1 Thess. 5:18, 24	1 Thess. 5:12, 13
22) 1 Tim. 1:4, 5	1 Tim. 1:3, 4, 5
23) 1 Tim. 5:20, 24, 25	1 Tim. 5:20, 22
24) James 5:12	James 5:8, 9, 12
25) 1 Pet. 4:8	1 Pet. 4:7, 8, 9, 10
26) 1 Pet. 5:5, 6	1 Pet. 5:5, 6
27) 1 John 1:7	1 John 1:7
28) 1 John 2:10	1 John 2:10

GOD'S CONDITIONAL PROMISES	RESPONSIBILITIES OF THE DOER OF THE WORD
29) 1 John 5:1	1 John 5:1
30) 1 John 5:16, 17	1 John 5:16
31) 3 John 6, 8	3 John 5, 6, 8
32.4) Matt. 10:19, 20, 22, 26, 32	Matt. 10:6, 7, 8, 12, 13, 16, 17, 19, 22, 26, 27, 28, 31, 32
33.4) 1 Cor. 8:8, 9, 12	1 Cor. 8:8, 9, 12, 13
34.4) Heb. 12:13	Heb. 12:12, 13

27 LIFE TOPIC   *The Return of Jesus*

PAGE 176	The end times, judgement, and rewards

GOD'S CONDITIONAL PROMISES	RESPONSIBILITIES OF THE DOER OF THE WORD
1) Matt. 10:41, 42	Matt. 10:41, 42
2) Matt. 16:27	Matt. 16:27
3) Matt. 24:13	Matt. 24:4, 13
4) Matt. 24:46, 47	Matt. 24:46
5) Matt. 25:34	Matt. 25:35, 36
6) Matt. 26:29	Matt. 26:26, 27
7) Mark 13:13	Mark 13:13, 33, 37
8) Luke 12:36, 37, 38, 40, 43, 48	Luke 12:35, 36, 37, 38, 40, 43, 48
9) Luke 14:14	Luke 14:13
10) Luke 20:35, 36	Luke 20:35
11) John 5:25	John 5:25
12) John 14:2, 3	John 14:1
13) Acts 17:27, 28, 30	Acts 17:27, 30
14) 1 Cor. 1:8	1 Cor. 1:7

GOD'S CONDITIONAL PROMISES	RESPONSIBILITIES OF THE DOER OF THE WORD
15) 1 Cor. 3:13, 14, 15	1 Cor. 3:14, 15
16) 1 Cor. 4:4, 5	1 Cor. 4:3, 4, 5
17) 1 Cor. 7:26, 28, 29, 31	1 Cor. 7:26, 27, 28, 29, 30, 31
18) 1 Cor. 11:26, 31, 32	1 Cor. 11:26, 28, 31, 33
19) 1 Cor. 15:22, 23, 24	1 Cor. 15:22, 23
20) 2 Cor. 5:10, 11	2 Cor. 5:9, 11
21) Phil. 3:20, 21	Phil. 3:20; 4:1
22) Col. 3:4, 10, 11	Col. 3:5, 8, 9, 10
23) 1 Thess. 4:14, 16	1 Thess. 4:14, 18
24) 2 Thess. 1:10	2 Thess. 1:10
25) 2 Thess. 2:3, 4	2 Thess. 2:2, 3
26) 2 Tim. 4:8	2 Tim. 4:8
27) Heb. 9:28	Heb. 9:28
28) James 5:8	James 5:8
29) 1 Pet. 2:12, 15	1 Pet. 2:11, 12, 13, 15, 16, 17
30) 1 Pet. 4:13	1 Pet. 4:12, 13
31) 1 Pet. 5:4	1 Pet. 5:2, 3
32) 1 Pet. 5:10	1 Pet. 5:10
33) 1 John 2:28	1 John 2:28
34) 2 John 8	2 John 8
35) Rev. 2:23, 26, 27, 28, 29	Rev. 2:19, 25, 26, 29
36) Rev. 3:8, 9, 10, 11, 12, 13	Rev. 3:8, 10, 11, 12, 13
37) Rev. 20:6	Rev. 20:6
38) Rev. 22:7, 14	Rev. 22:7, 14
39.4) Prov. 27:18	Prov. 27:18
40.4) Isa. 28:5, 6	Isa. 28:5, 6
41) Isa. 66:11, 12, 13, 14, 22, 24	Isa. 66:10

28 LIFE TOPIC   *Hearing and Obeying*

PAGE 184	God's calling, purpose, and destiny for your life

GOD'S CONDITIONAL PROMISES	RESPONSIBILITIES OF THE DOER OF THE WORD
1) 1 Kgs. 11:38	1 Kgs. 11:38
2) Mark 1:17	Mark 1:17
3) Luke 9:23, 24	Luke 9:23, 24
4) Luke 9:62	Luke 9:59, 60
5) Luke 17:20, 21, 33	Luke 17:33
6) John 14:12	John 14:12
7) Acts 20:24	Acts 20:24
8) Rom. 12:2	Rom. 12:1, 2
9) 1 Cor. 2:10, 11, 12	1 Cor. 2:13
10) 1 Cor. 3:8, 9	1 Cor. 3:8, 9, 10
11) 2 Cor. 5:18, 19, 21	2 Cor. 5:18, 19, 20
12) 2 Cor. 12:12, 15	2 Cor. 12:12, 14, 15, 19, 21
13) Col. 1:25, 27, 28	Col. 1:25, 28
14) Col. 4:17	Col. 4:17
15) 1 Tim. 3:1	1 Tim. 3:1, 2, 3, 4, 6, 7
16) 1 Tim. 4:15, 16	1 Tim. 4:12, 13, 14, 15, 16
17) Heb. 5:4	Heb. 5:4

29 LIFE TOPIC   *Evil*

PAGE 190	Authority over demons and works of darkness

GOD'S CONDITIONAL PROMISES	RESPONSIBILITIES OF THE DOER OF THE WORD
1) Mark 9:29	Mark 9:29

GOD'S CONDITIONAL PROMISES	RESPONSIBILITIES OF THE DOER OF THE WORD
2) Mark 9:39, 40	Mark 9:39, 40
3) Rom. 8:38, 39	Rom. 8:38
4) 2 Cor. 10:3, 4, 6	2 Cor. 10:3, 4, 5, 6
5) Eph. 6:10, 11, 12, 13	Eph. 6:10, 11, 13, 14, 15, 16, 17, 18
6) James 4:7	James 4:7

30 LIFE TOPIC   *Being God's Friend*

PAGE 194	Pleasing and honoring him

GOD'S CONDITIONAL PROMISES	RESPONSIBILITIES OF THE DOER OF THE WORD
1) 1 Sam. 2:30	1 Sam. 2:30
2) Ps. 24:5	Ps. 24:4, 6
3) Ps. 33:5	Ps. 33:5
4) Ps. 50:23	Ps. 50:23
5) Ps. 63:8, 11	Ps. 63:1, 3, 4, 5, 6, 7, 8, 11
6) Prov. 23:15, 16	Prov. 23:15, 16
7) Matt. 5:8	Matt. 5:8
8) Matt. 11:6	Matt. 11:6
9) John 8:31, 32	John 8:31
10) John 15:9, 10, 11, 12, 13, 14, 15	John 15:9, 10, 12, 13, 14
11) 1 Cor. 8:3, 4, 6	1 Cor. 8:3, 6
12) 2 Cor. 10:18	2 Cor. 10:17
13) Heb. 11:6	Heb. 11:6
14) Heb. 13:16	Heb. 13:16
15) James 4:2, 3, 4, 5, 6	James 4:2, 3, 4, 6
16) 1 John 4:7, 11	1 John 4:7, 11

GOD'S CONDITIONAL PROMISES	RESPONSIBILITIES OF THE DOER OF THE WORD
17) 3 John 11	3 John 11
18.4) Ex. 19:5, 6	Ex. 19:5

31 LIFE TOPIC   *Spirit-filled Living*

PAGE 200	Working out your own salvation through spiritual gifts with power

GOD'S CONDITIONAL PROMISES	RESPONSIBILITIES OF THE DOER OF THE WORD
1) Matt. 21:43	Matt. 21:43
2) Acts 1:5, 8	Acts 1:8
3) Acts 2:38, 39	Acts 2:38
4) Rom. 8:9, 10, 11, 13	Rom. 8:9, 10, 11, 13
5) Phil. 1:6	Phil. 1:6
6.4) Isa. 57:13	Isa. 57:13
7.4) 2 Tim. 2:20, 21	2 Tim. 2:21

32 LIFE TOPIC   *Grace vs. Law*

PAGE 204	Being righteous in Christ, free from sin and the curse of the law

GOD'S CONDITIONAL PROMISES	RESPONSIBILITIES OF THE DOER OF THE WORD
1) Rom. 3:28; 4:5, 16	Rom. 3:28; 4:5, 12, 16
2) Rom. 5:17, 20, 21	Rom. 5:17
3) Rom. 6:7, 8, 9, 12, 14, 23	Rom. 6:7, 8, 9, 11, 12, 13
4) Rom. 7:4, 6	Rom. 7:4, 6

GOD'S CONDITIONAL PROMISES	RESPONSIBILITIES OF THE DOER OF THE WORD
5) Rom. 8:1, 2, 3, 4	Rom. 8:1, 4
6) Rom. 10:4	Rom. 10:4
7) Rom. 13:8, 10	Rom. 13:8, 9, 10
8) Gal. 3:11, 12, 13, 14	Gal. 3:11, 14
9) Gal. 3:24, 25	Gal. 3:24
10) Gal. 4:28, 31; 5:6	Gal. 5:1, 5, 6
11) Gal. 5:18, 19, 22, 23	Gal. 5:18, 22, 23
12) Phil. 3:8, 9	Phil. 3:7, 8, 9
13) 1 Tim. 1:8, 9, 10, 11	1 Tim. 1:8
14) James 2:10, 13	James 2:10, 12
15.4) 2 Cor. 3:3, 6	2 Cor. 3:4, 5
16.4) Phil. 3:3	Phil. 3:1, 2, 3

33 LIFE TOPIC   *Spiritual Gifts*

PAGE 210	For service and ministry to others

GOD'S CONDITIONAL PROMISES	RESPONSIBILITIES OF THE DOER OF THE WORD
1) Rom. 10:17	Rom. 10:17
2) Rom. 12:3, 4, 5, 6, 7, 8	Rom. 12:3, 6, 7, 8
3) 1 Cor. 1:7, 8	1 Cor. 1:7
4) 1 Cor. 12:3	1 Cor. 12:3
5) 1 Cor. 14:2, 3, 4, 5	1 Cor. 14:1, 2, 3, 4, 5, 13
6) 1 Cor. 14:33	1 Cor. 14:26, 33, 40
7) Phil. 2:13	Phil. 2:12
8) Phil. 3:12, 15	Phil. 3:12, 13, 14, 15, 16

GOD'S CONDITIONAL PROMISES	RESPONSIBILITIES OF THE DOER OF THE WORD
9) 1 Thess. 2:13	1 Thess. 2:13
10) James 2:17, 20, 22, 24, 26	James 2:17, 22, 24, 26
11) 1 Pet. 4:11	1 Pet. 4:10, 11

Reflection Notes

APPENDIX
B

Appendix B is a directory for locating
God's Conditional Promises by Bible
Books / Chapters / Verses.

To search for God's Conditional Promises
by Life Topic, see Appendix A.

In this Appendix B, however, you will find
the Conditional Promises located in the
Unabridged Edition have been added, and
are highlighted in gray for additional studies.

Since this book is the *Condensed Edition* of *The Conditional Promises of God,* not all of the Conditional Promises of God regarding His blessings are printed in their expanded form, as they are in the *Unabridged Edition.*

Note that Life Topics 1 and 14 are omitted from the Condensed Edition, and are found in their entirety in the Unabridged Edition.

— How to Use Appendix B —

Key to Abbreviations

No.   Sequential numbering of all the conditional promises, in biblical order

LT   Life Topic Number

Loc #   Location of the Conditional Promise within the Life Topic

C.P.   Number of Conditional Promises found in this passage

Cndt.   Number of conditions for the doer of the Word found in this passage

Pg.   Page number where this Conditional Promise is located

NOTE: The C.P., and Cndt. Columns, and Page Numbers have been left blank.

As you study the various passages, you may write the number of promises in the C.P. column, and the Number of Conditions in the Cndt. column and the Page where you found it.

NO.	LT	LOC #	CONDITIONAL PROMISES	C.P.	DOER OF THE WORD	CNDT	PG.
PSALMS							
55	8	5)	Ps. 1:1, 3	2	Ps. 1:1-2	5	
56	7	51.4)	Ps. 2:8, 12		Ps. 2:8, 10-12		
57	11	5)	Ps. 3:3, 5, 7-8		Ps. 3:4-6		
58	12	1)	Ps. 4:1	1	Ps. 4:1	1	

Conditional Promises Directory by Books of the Bible

THE BOOKS OF THE OLD TESTAMENT

Book	Abbr.	Book	Abbr.
Genesis	Gen.	Ecclesiastes	Eccl.
Exodus	Ex.	The Song of Solomon	Song
Leviticus	Lev.	Isaiah	Isa.
Numbers	Num.	Jeremiah	Jer.
Deuteronomy	Deut.	Lamentations	Lam.
Joshua	Josh.	Ezekiel	Ezek.
Judges	Judg.	Daniel	Dan.
Ruth	Ruth	Hosea	Hos.
1 Samuel	1 Sam.	Joel	Joel
2 Samuel	2 Sam.	Amos	Amos
1 Kings	1 Kgs.	Obadiah	Obad.
2 Kings	2 Kgs.	Jonah	Jon.
1 Chronicles	1 Chron.	Micah	Mic.
2 Chronicles	2 Chron.	Nahum	Nah.
Ezra	Ezra	Habakkuk	Hab.
Nehemiah	Neh.	Zephaniah	Zeph.
Esther	Esth.	Haggai	Hag.
Job	Job	Zechariah	Zech.
Psalms	Ps.	Malachi	Mal.
Proverbs	Prov.		

THE BOOKS OF THE NEW TESTAMENT

Book	Abbr.	Book	Abbr.
Matthew	Matt.	1 Timothy	1 Tim.
Mark	Mark	2 Timothy	2 Tim.
Luke	Luke	Titus	Titus
John	John	Philemon	Philem.
Acts	Acts	Hebrews	Heb.
Romans	Rom.	James	James
1 Corinthians	1 Cor.	1 Peter	1 Pet.
2 Corinthians	2 Cor.	2 Peter	2 Pet.
Galatians	Gal.	1 John	1 John
Ephesians	Eph.	2 John	2 John
Philippians	Phil.	3 John	3 John
Colossians	Col.	Jude	Jude
1 Thessalonians	1 Thess.	Revelation	Rev.
2 Thessalonians	2 Thess.		

Reflection Notes

NO.	LT	LOC #	CONDITIONAL PROMISES	C.P.	DOER OF THE WORD	CNDT	PG.
			GENESIS				
I	I	1)	Gen. 1:26		Gen. 1:28		
2	2	22.4)	Gen. 2:18, 24-25		Gen. 2:23-24		
3	3	1)	Gen. 4:7		Gen. 4:7		
4	15	49.4)	Gen. 7:1, 9-10, 16		Gen. 7:1, 5, 7		
5	5	141.4)	Gen. 12:2-3		Gen. 12:1		
6	5	1)	Gen. 15:1, 6		Gen. 15:1, 6		
7	5	2)	Gen. 17:2, 4, 6		Gen. 17:1		
8	25	24.4)	Gen. 17:2, 4, 6		Gen. 17:1		
9	2	23.4)	Gen. 17:7		Gen. 17:1, 9-10		
10	2	24.4)	Gen. 22:16-18		Gen. 22:2-3, 9-12, 18		
11	8	49.4)	Gen. 22:16-18		Gen. 22:2-3, 9-12, 18		
11	7	(11 C.P. found in 7 Life Topics)					
			EXODUS				
12	21	56.4)	Ex. 12:13, 43		Ex. 12:43, 48		
13	6	1)	Ex. 15:26		Ex. 15:26		
14	7	47.4)	Ex. 18:19, 23		Ex. 18:19-21, 23		
15	30	18.4)	Ex. 19:5-6	4	Ex. 19:5	2	199
16	6	2)	Ex. 20:6, 12, 24		Ex. 20:6, 12		
17	18	1)	Ex. 20:6, 12, 24		Ex. 20:6, 12		
18	5	3)	Ex. 20:6, 24		Ex. 20:3-7, 13-17, 23		
7	6	(7 C.P. found in 6 Life Topics)					
			DEUTERONOMY				
19	2	1)	Deut. 4:40		Deut. 4:39-40		
20	6	3)	Deut. 4:40		Deut. 4:39-40		

NO.	LT	LOC #	CONDITIONAL PROMISES	C.P.	DOER OF THE WORD	CNDT	PG.
21	8	1)	Deut. 4:40		Deut. 4:39-40		
22	6	47.4)	Deut. 11:8-9, 16		Deut. 11:8, 16		
23	7	48.4)	Deut. 11:8, 13-14, 16		Deut. 11:8, 13, 16		
24	5	142.4)	Deut. 11:16, 26-27		Deut. 11:1, 8, 16, 27, 32		
25	8	50.4)	Deut. 15:4-6		Deut. 15:1-3, 5-6		
26	3	2)	Deut. 15:10		Deut. 15:7-11		
27	7	49.4)	Deut. 28:1		Deut. 28:1		
28	6	4)	Deut. 28:1-2, 4		Deut. 28:1-2		
29	8	51.4)	Deut. 28:1-2, 4-5		Deut. 28:1-2		
30	7	1)	Deut. 28:1-2, 6		Deut. 28:1-2		
31	5	4)	Deut. 28:1-3		Deut. 28:1-2		
32	11	1)	Deut. 28:1, 7		Deut. 28:1		
33	8	2)	Deut. 28:1, 8		Deut. 28:1		
34	5	5)	Deut. 28:9-10		Deut. 28:9		
35	6	5)	Deut. 28:9, 11		Deut. 28:9		
36	8	52.4)	Deut. 28:9, 11-12		Deut. 28:9, 12		
37	7	2)	Deut. 28:13		Deut. 28:13-14		
38	2	2)	Deut. 30:5-6, 10		Deut. 30:2, 8, 10		
39	8	3)	Deut. 30:5, 10		Deut. 30:2, 8, 10		
40	9	1)	Deut. 30:5, 10		Deut. 30:2, 8, 10		
41	11	2)	Deut. 30:7, 10		Deut. 30:2, 8, 10		
23	8	(23 C.P. found in 8 Life Topics)					

NO.	LT	LOC #	CONDITIONAL PROMISES	C.P.	DOER OF THE WORD	CNDT	PG.
			JOSHUA				
42	8	4)	Josh. 1:5, 7-9		Josh. 1:6-9		
43	2	25.4)	Josh. 14:9		Josh. 14:9		
2	2	(2 C.P. found in 2 Life Topics)					
			1 SAMUEL				
44	30	1)	1 Sam. 2:30	2	1 Sam. 2:30	1	196
45	7	50.4)	1 Sam. 24:19-20; 26:25		1 Sam. 24:6		
2	2	(2 C.P. found in 2 Life Topics)					
			2 SAMUEL				
46	11	44.4)	2 Sam. 22:2-4, 18-20, 48-49		2 Sam. 22:3-4, 7, 22-24, 38-39, 50		
47	5	6)	2 Sam. 22:26-28		2 Sam. 22:26-28		
2	2	(2 C.P. found in 2 Life Topics)					
			1 KINGS				
48	5	143.4)	1 Kgs. 6:12-13; 9:3-4		1 Kgs. 6:12; 9:4		
49	28	1)	1 Kgs. 11:38		1 Kgs. 11:38		
2	2	(2 C.P. found in 2 Life Topics)					
			2 CHRONICLES				
50	8	53.4)	2 Chron. 7:14		2 Chron. 7:14		
51	7	3)	2 Chron. 15:2, 7		2 Chron. 15:2, 7		
52	11	3)	2 Chron. 16:9	1	2 Chron. 16:9	1	86
53	11	4)	2 Chron. 20:9, 15, 17, 20		2 Chron. 20:3-4, 9, 12, 15, 17-21		
4	3	(4 C.P. found in 3 Life Topics)					

NO.	LT	LOC #	CONDITIONAL PROMISES	C.P.	DOER OF THE WORD	CNDT	PG.
			JOB				
54	17	1)	Job 28:28	3	Job 28:28	2	118
1	1	(1 C.P. found in 1 Life Topics)					
			PSALMS				
55	8	5)	Ps. 1:1, 3	2	Ps. 1:1-2	5	68
56	7	51.4)	Ps. 2:8, 12		Ps. 2:8, 10-12		
57	11	5)	Ps. 3:3, 5, 7-8		Ps. 3:4-6		
58	12	1)	Ps. 4:1	1	Ps. 4:1	1	92
59	5	7)	Ps. 4:3	1	Ps. 4:3	1	46
60	12	2)	Ps. 4:7-8		Ps. 4:4-5, 8		
61	11	6)	Ps. 5:4-6, 11-12		Ps. 5:7, 11-12		
62	11	7)	Ps. 7:8-11		Ps. 7:10, 17		
63	1	5.4)	Ps. 8:4-8		Ps. 8:3		
64	11	8)	Ps. 9:9-10, 12-13		Ps. 9:1-2, 10-12, 14		
65	13	1)	Ps. 9:18	1	Ps. 9:18	1	100
66	12	3)	Ps. 10:14, 17-18		Ps. 10:14, 17		
67	13	2)	Ps. 10:14, 17-18	5	Ps. 10:14, 17	2	100
68	5	144.4)	Ps. 11:5, 7		Ps. 11:1, 5, 7		
69	13	3)	Ps. 12:5; 14:6	4	Ps. 13:5-6	3	100
70	5	8)	Ps. 15:1-5		Ps. 15:2-5		
71	8	6)	Ps. 15:5		Ps. 15:5		
72	12	4)	Ps. 16:5-11		Ps. 16:1, 7-8		
73	11	9)	Ps. 17:6-7, 18:1-3		Ps. 17:3-4, 6-7; 18:1-3, 6		
74	5	9)	Ps. 18:25-27		Ps. 18:25-27		
75	7	52.4)	Ps. 18:28-30		Ps. 18:30		
76	11	10)	Ps. 18:32-34, 47-48, 50		Ps. 18:49		

NO.	LT	LOC #	CONDITIONAL PROMISES	C.P.	DOER OF THE WORD	CNDT	PG.
77	5	10)	Ps. 19:7-9		Ps. 19:7, 10, 14		
78	11	11)	Ps. 20:6	2	Ps. 20:7-8	2	86
79	8	54.4)	Ps. 23:1		Ps. 23: 1, 4		
80	12	54.4)	Ps. 23:1-4, 6		Ps. 23: 1, 4		
81	30	2)	Ps. 24:5		Ps. 24:4, 6		
82	11	12)	Ps. 25:2		Ps. 25: 1-2, 5		
83	7	4)	Ps. 25: 3, 9-10		Ps. 25: 1-3, 5, 9-10		
84	2	3)	Ps. 25:12, 13, 14	4	Ps. 25:12, 14	2	32
85	8	7)	Ps. 25:12-14		Ps. 25:12, 14		
86	11	45.4)	Ps. 25:15		Ps. 25:15		
87	12	55.4)	Ps. 27:1, 5-6, 14		Ps. 27:3, 6, 14		
88	24	1)	Ps. 28:8		Ps. 28:1, 7		
89	12	5)	Ps. 29:11		Ps. 1-2		
90	12	6)	Ps. 30:5		Ps. 30:1, 4, 12		
91	12	7)	Ps. 31:3-4, 15, 19-20, 23-24		Ps. 31:1, 5, 19, 23-24		
92	19	1)	Ps. 32:1-2		Ps. 32:2		
93	24	1)	Ps. 32:7-8, 10		Ps. 32:5, 10-11		
94	30	3)	Ps. 33:5	1	Ps. 33:5	2	196
95	5	11)	Ps. 33:12, 20-21		Ps. 33:12, 20-21		
96	8	8)	Ps. 33:18-19		Ps. 33:18		
97	14	1)	Ps. 34:7		Ps. 34:7		
98	5	12)	Ps. 34:8		Ps. 34:8-9		
99	8	9)	Ps. 34:9, 10	3	Ps. 34:9, 10	2	68
100	6	6)	Ps. 34:12		Ps. 34:13-14		
101	9	2)	Ps. 34:15, 17-18		Ps. 34:15, 17-18		
102	15	1)	Ps. 34:19-20, 22		Ps. 34:19, 22		

NO.	LT	LOC #	CONDITIONAL PROMISES	C.P.	DOER OF THE WORD	CNDT	PG.
103	8	10)	Ps. 36:8		Ps. 36:7		
104	6	7)	Ps. 36:9	1	Ps. 36:7	1	56
105	17	2)	Ps. 36:9		Ps. 36:7		
106	5	13)	Ps. 37:4-5		Ps. 37:3-5		
107	7	5)	Ps. 37:4-5		Ps. 37:3-5		
108	8	11)	Ps. 37:4-5		Ps. 37:3-5		
109	12	8)	Ps. 37:4-5	2	Ps. 37:3-5	7	92
110	15	2)	Ps. 37:4-6		Ps. 37:3-5		
111	1	2)	Ps. 37:9, 11		Ps. 37:7- 9, 11		
112	8	12)	Ps. 37:17, 19, 29, 31		Ps. 37:17, 21, 27, 31		
113	16	1)	Ps. 37:18	2	Ps. 37:18	1	114
114	17	3)	Ps. 37:30	2	Ps. 37:30	1	118
115	15	3)	Ps. 37:32-34		Ps. 37:32, 34		
116	11	13)	Ps. 37:39-40		Ps. 37:39-40		
117	5	14)	Ps. 40:4	1	Ps. 40:4	3	46
118	5	15)	Ps. 40:17		Ps. 40:1, 8-10		
119	6	8)	Ps. 41:1-3		Ps. 41:1		
120	5	145.4)	Ps. 41:10-12		Ps. 41:4, 10		
121	11	14)	Ps. 42:8		Ps. 42:11		
122	12	9)	Ps. 43:2, 5		Ps. 43:4-5		
123	11	15)	Ps. 46:1, 7	5	Ps. 46:2	1	86
124	16	16.4)	Ps. 48:14		Ps. 48:9		
125	16	2)	Ps. 49:15	2	Ps. 49:5	1	114
126	12	10)	Ps. 50:15	2	Ps. 50:15	1	92
127	30	4)	Ps. 50:23	2	Ps. 50:23	1	196
128	9	3)	Ps. 51:17	1	Ps. 51:3, 17	4	76
129	11	16)	Ps. 55:16-17, 22		Ps. 55:16-17, 22-23		

NO.	LT	LOC #	CONDITIONAL PROMISES	C.P.	DOER OF THE WORD	CNDT	PG.
130	12	11)	Ps. 56:8-9		Ps. 56:3-4, 10-12		
131	11	17)	Ps. 57:2-3		Ps. 57:1-2, 6-7, 9		
132	11	18)	Ps. 59:9-11, 17		Ps. 59:9, 16-17		
133	5	16)	Ps. 62:12		Ps. 62:1, 8, 10		
134	30	5)	Ps. 63:8, 11		Ps. 63:1, 3-8, 11		
135	15	4)	Ps. 64:10		Ps. 64:10		
136	5	146.4)	Ps. 65:4		Ps. 65:4		
137	5	17)	Ps. 67:4		Ps. 67:3-4		
138	1	3)	Ps. 67:6-7		Ps. 67:5		
139	13	4)	Ps. 68:5-6		Ps. 68:4		
140	13	5)	Ps. 69:32-33		Ps. 69:30, 32		
141	19	63.4)	Ps. 69:35-36		Ps. 69:36		
142	11	19)	Ps. 71:3, 5, 7, 20-21, 23		Ps. 71:1, 8, 14-16, 22-24		
143	5	18)	Ps. 73:1		Ps. 73:1		
144	12	12)	Ps. 73:23-24, 26, 28		Ps. 73:25, 28		
145	5	147.4)	Ps. 75:10		Ps. 75:1, 9-10		
146	5	148.4)	Ps. 81:8, 10		Ps. 81:8-10		
147	5	19)	Ps. 84:4		Ps. 84:2, 4		
148	12	13)	Ps. 84:5-7, 11-12		Ps. 84:2, 4-5, 11-12		
149	8	13)	Ps. 84:11-12		Ps. 84:2, 4-5, 11-12		
150	8	14)	Ps. 85:8-9, 12-13		Ps. 85:8-9		
151	5	20)	Ps. 86:5	3	Ps. 86:5	1	46
152	5	149.4)	Ps. 89:15-17		Ps. 89:15-16		

NO.	LT	LOC #	CONDITIONAL PROMISES	C.P.	DOER OF THE WORD	CNDT	PG.
153	11	20)	Ps. 91:1, 9-12, 14-15		Ps. 91:1-2, 9, 14-15		
154	8	15)	Ps. 91:9-10		Ps. 91:2, 9		
155	1	6.4)	Ps. 91:13		Ps. 91:2, 9		
156	6	9)	Ps. 91:16	1	Ps. 91:2, 9	5	56
157	21	1)	Ps. 91:16		Ps. 91:2, 9		
158	11	21)	Ps. 92:4		Ps. 92:1-3		
159	6	10)	Ps. 92:12-15		Ps. 92:12-13		
160	12	14)	Ps. 94:12-15, 18-19		Ps. 94:12, 15		
161	5	21)	Ps. 96:13		Ps. 96:1-3, 8-10		
162	11	22)	Ps. 97:10, 11		Ps. 97:10-12		
163	5	22)	Ps. 98:9		Ps. 98:1, 4, 6		
164	5	23)	Ps. 100:5		Ps. 100:1, 4		
165	2	26.4)	Ps. 102:12-13, 16, 18, 28		Ps. 102:14-15, 18		
166	13	6)	Ps. 102:17	2	Ps. 102:17	1	100
167	6	11)	Ps. 103:3, 5		Ps. 103:1, 2		
168	5	24)	Ps. 103:6, 11, 13		Ps. 103:11, 13		
169	6	12)	Ps. 103:17		Ps. 103:17-18		
170	2	4)	Ps. 103:17-18		Ps. 103:18		
171	5	25)	Ps. 106:3	2	Ps. 106:3	2	46
172	5	26)	Ps. 107:9, 43		Ps. 107:1-2, 8-9, 22, 32, 43		
173	13	7)	Ps. 107:41, 43		Ps. 107:42, 43		
174	11	23)	Ps. 108:13		Ps. 108:1, 3		
175	15	5)	Ps. 109:31		Ps. 109:30		
176	17	4)	Ps. 111:10		Ps. 111:1, 10		
177	3	3)	Ps. 112:1	1	Ps. 112:1, 9	4	36

NO.	LT	LOC #	CONDITIONAL PROMISES	C.P.	DOER OF THE WORD	CNDT	PG.
178	2	5)	Ps. 112:1-2		Ps. 112:1-2, 4-5, 7		
179	8	16)	Ps. 112:1, 3		Ps. 112:1, 4-5, 7		
180	5	27)	Ps. 112:1, 3-4, 9		Ps. 112:1, 4-5, 7		
181	13	8)	Ps. 113:7-9		Ps. 113:1, 3		
182	15	6)	Ps. 115:11	2	Ps. 115:11	2	106
183	7	6)	Ps. 115:13	2	Ps. 115:13	1	64
184	10	1)	Ps. 115:13	2	Ps. 115:13	1	82
185	18	2)	Ps. 115:13	2	Ps. 115:13	1	124
186	15	7)	Ps. 115:13		Ps. 115:13		
187	13	9)	Ps. 116:6		Ps. 116:6, 9, 13-14, 17		
188	9	26.4)	Ps. 116:15		Ps. 116:15		
189	16	3)	Ps. 116:15	1	Ps. 116:15	1	114
190	5	28)	Ps. 117:2		Ps. 117:1		
191	12	56.4)	Ps. 118:6, 14		Ps. 118:6, 8-9		
192	16	4)	Ps. 118:20	2	Ps. 118:20	1	114
193	5	29)	Ps. 118:26	1	Ps. 118:26	1	46
194	12	15)	Ps. 119:1-2		Ps. 119:1-4, 7-8, 15-16, 24		
195	7	7)	Ps. 119:32		Ps. 119:27, 30-35		
196	8	17)	Ps. 119:72		Ps. 119:67, 69-70		
197	5	30)	Ps. 119:74		Ps. 119:74		
198	15	8)	Ps. 119:86	1	Ps. 119:81, 83	2	102
199	11	24)	Ps. 119:98		Ps. 119:97, 99-100		
200	5	31)	Ps. 119:101, 103-104		Ps. 119:101-102, 104		

NO.	LT	LOC #	CONDITIONAL PROMISES	C.P.	DOER OF THE WORD	CNDT	PG.
201	7	8)	Ps. 119:105		Ps. 119:106		
202	12	16)	Ps. 119:114	2	Ps. 119:114-115	2	92
203	7	9)	Ps. 119:165		Ps. 119:165-168		
204	5	32)	Ps. 119:171		Ps. 119:171-174, 176		
205	12	57.4)	Ps. 121:2-3, 5, 7-8		Ps. 121:1		
206	11	46.4)	Ps. 125:1-2		Ps. 125:1		
207	22	24.4)	Ps. 125:3-4		Ps. 125:3-4		
208	9	27.4)	Ps. 126:5-6		Ps. 126:5-6		
209	7	10)	Ps. 127:1	1	Ps. 127:1	1	64
210	7	11)	Ps. 127:1		Ps. 127:1		
211	12	17)	Ps. 127:2		Ps. 127:2		
212	2	6)	Ps. 127:5		Ps. 127:5		
213	5	33)	Ps. 128:1	1	Ps. 128:1	2	46
214	8	18)	Ps. 128:2	2	Ps. 128:2	1	68
215	2	7)	Ps. 128:3, 4, 6	4	Ps. 128:4	1	32
216	21	57.4)	Ps. 130:7-8		Ps. 130:1, 5-6		
217	11	25)	Ps. 138:6-7		Ps. 138:1-2		
218	6	48.4)	Ps. 138:8		Ps. 138:1-2		
219	12	18)	Ps. 139:10		Ps. 139:14		
220	13	10)	Ps. 140:12		Ps. 140:6, 13		
221	12	19)	Ps. 144:15	2	Ps. 144:9, 15	4	93
222	2	8)	Ps. 145:4		Ps. 145:1-2, 5-7		
223	9	4)	Ps. 145:14-15		Ps. 145:10-12, 15		
224	13	11)	Ps. 145:14-16		Ps. 145:10-12, 15		
225	12	20)	Ps. 145:18	2	Ps. 145:18	2	93
226	6	13)	Ps. 145:19-20		Ps. 145:19-21		

NO.	LT	LOC #	CONDITIONAL PROMISES	C.P.	DOER OF THE WORD	CNDT	PG.
227	12	21)	Ps. 145:19-20		Ps. 145:19-21		
228	13	12)	Ps. 145:19-20		Ps. 145:19-21		
229	5	34)	Ps. 146:5	1	Ps. 146:5	2	47
230	15	9)	Ps. 146:5, 7		Ps. 146:2, 5		
231	13	13)	Ps. 146:5, 7, 9		Ps. 146:2, 5		
232	5	35)	Ps. 146:8	1	Ps. 146:8	1	47
233	6	14)	Ps. 146:8		Ps. 146:2		
234	12	22)	Ps. 146:8		Ps. 146:2, 8		
235	21	2)	Ps. 146:8		Ps. 146:2		
236	12	23)	Ps. 147:3	2	Ps. 147:1	1	93
237	7	12)	Ps. 147:6	1	Ps. 147:6	1	64
238	5	36)	Ps. 147:11	2	Ps. 147:11	2	47
239	19	2)	Ps. 149:4	3	Ps. 149:4	2	132
186	24	(186 C.P. found in 24 Life Topics)					
PROVERBS							
240	17	5)	Prov. 1:2-7		Prov. 1:7		
241	18	3)	Prov. 1:2-7		Prov. 1:7		
242	18	34.4)	Prov. 1:9	2	Prov. 1:8	2	129
243	5	150.4)	Prov. 1:33		Prov. 1:33		
244	17	6)	Prov. 2:1, 5, 7		Prov. 2:1-4, 7		
245	11	26)	Prov. 2:7-8	3	Prov. 2:7	1	87
246	5	37)	Prov. 2:9		Prov. 2:7		
247	18	4)	Prov. 2:11-17, 20		Prov. 2:10-11		
248	5	38)	Prov. 2:21	2	Prov. 2:21	2	47
249	6	15)	Prov. 3:2	3	Prov. 3:1	2	56
250	5	39)	Prov. 3:4		Prov. 3:3		
251	17	7)	Prov. 3:6	1	Prov. 3:5-6	3	118

NO.	LT	LOC #	CONDITIONAL PROMISES	C.P.	DOER OF THE WORD	CNDT	PG.
252	6	16)	Prov. 3:8	2	Prov. 3:7	3	57
253	3	4)	Prov. 3:10	2	Prov. 3:9	2	36
254	9	5)	Prov. 3:12	1	Prov. 3:11	2	76
255	17	8)	Prov. 3:13, 18	3	Prov. 3:13, 18	4	118
256	5	40)	Prov. 3:22-24		Prov. 3:21		
257	11	27)	Prov. 3:26	2	Prov. 3:25	2	87
258	5	41)	Prov. 3:33-35	3	Prov. 3:33-35	3	47
259	17	9)	Prov. 4:6, 8-9		Prov. 4:1-2, 4-8		
260	6	17)	Prov. 4:10	1	Prov. 4:10	2	57
261	7	13)	Prov. 4:12-13		Prov. 4:13		
262	6	18)	Prov. 4:22		Prov. 4:20-22		
263	18	5)	Prov. 5:2		Prov. 5:1		
264	18	6)	Prov. 6:22		Prov. 6:20-21		
265	17	10)	Prov. 8:9		Prov. 8:9		
266	8	19)	Prov. 8:9, 11		Prov. 8:9-10		
267	7	53.4)	Prov. 8:17		Prov. 8:17		
268	8	55.4)	Prov. 8:20-21		Prov. 8:21		
269	5	42)	Prov. 8:32, 34-35		Prov. 8:32-35		
270	17	11)	Prov. 9:10	2	Prov. 9:10	2	119
271	6	19)	Prov. 9:11-12	3	Prov. 9:12	1	57
272	19	3)	Prov. 10:2	1	Prov. 10:2	1	132
273	6	20)	Prov. 10:3	2	Prov. 10:3	1	57
274	8	20)	Prov. 10:4-5	3	Prov. 10:4-5	2	69
275	5	43)	Prov. 10:6-7	2	Prov. 10:6	1	47
276	6	21)	Prov. 10:27-29		Prov. 10:27-29		
277	7	14)	Prov. 10:30-32		Prov. 10:30-32		
278	17	12)	Prov. 11:2	2	Prov. 11:2	1	119

NO.	LT	LOC #	CONDITIONAL PROMISES	C.P.	DOER OF THE WORD	CNDT	PG.
279	7	15)	Prov. 11:3	2	Prov. 11:3	1	64
280	12	24)	Prov. 11:4-6, 8		Prov. 11:4-6, 8		
281	5	44)	Prov. 11:9		Prov. 11:9		
282	17	13)	Prov. 11:14	1	Prov. 11:14	1	119
283	8	21)	Prov. 11:15	2	Prov. 11:15	1	69
284	5	45)	Prov. 11:18	2	Prov. 11:18	1	48
285	3	5)	Prov. 11:25	3	Prov. 11:25	2	36
286	5	46)	Prov. 11:27-28, 30		Prov. 11:27-28, 30		
287	5	47)	Prov. 12:2-3, 7		Prov. 12:2-3, 7		
288	12	25)	Prov. 12:6	2	Prov. 12:6	1	93
289	17	14)	Prov. 12:8	1	Prov. 12:8	1	119
290	8	22)	Prov. 12:11-12	4	Prov. 12:11-12	2	69
291	11	28)	Prov. 12:13	1	Prov. 12:13	1	87
292	8	23)	Prov. 12:14	3	Prov. 12:14	2	69
293	5	48)	Prov. 12:19	1	Prov. 12:19	1	48
294	12	26)	Prov. 12:20-21	2	Prov. 12:20-21	2	93
295	5	49)	Prov. 12:22	2	Prov. 12:22	1	48
296	7	16)	Prov. 12:24	2	Prov. 12:24	1	64
297	10	2)	Prov. 12:28	3	Prov. 12:28	1	82
298	8	24)	Prov. 13:2	1	Prov. 13:2	1	69
299	6	22)	Prov. 13:3	2	Prov. 13:3	1	58
300	8	25)	Prov. 13:4	2	Prov. 13:4	1	70
301	13	14)	Prov. 13:6	1	Prov. 13:6	1	101
302	17	15)	Prov. 13:10	2	Prov. 13:10	1	119
303	8	26)	Prov. 13:11	2	Prov. 13:11	1	70
304	5	50)	Prov. 13:13	2	Prov. 13:13	1	48
305	17	16)	Prov. 13:15	1	Prov. 13:15	1	120

NO.	LT	LOC #	CONDITIONAL PROMISES	C.P.	DOER OF THE WORD	CNDT	PG.
306	5	51)	Prov. 13:18	2	Prov. 13:18	1	48
307	12	27)	Prov. 13:21	1	Prov. 13:21	1	94
308	17	17)	Prov. 14:6	1	Prov. 14:6	1	120
309	8	27)	Prov. 14:11	2	Prov. 14:11	1	70
310	7	17)	Prov. 14:14		Prov. 14:14		
311	17	18)	Prov. 14:18	1	Prov. 14:18	1	120
312	5	52)	Prov. 14:19		Prov. 14:19		
313	3	6)	Prov. 14:21	2	Prov. 14:21	1	36
314	18	7)	Prov. 14:22	1	Prov. 14:22	1	126
315	8	28)	Prov. 14:23	1	Prov. 14:23	1	70
316	18	8)	Prov. 14:26		Prov. 14:26		
317	22	1)	Prov. 14:27		Prov. 14:27		
318	6	49.4)	Prov. 14:30		Prov. 14:30		
319	6	23)	Prov. 15:4	1	Prov. 15:4	1	58
320	18	9)	Prov. 15:5	2	Prov. 15:5	1	126
321	8	29)	Prov. 15:6	2	Prov. 15:6	1	70
322	5	53)	Prov. 15:8-9	3	Prov. 15:8-9	2	48
323	6	24)	Prov. 15:13, 15	3	Prov. 15:13, 15	2	58
324	7	18)	Prov. 15:19	2	Prov. 15:19	1	64
325	5	54)	Prov. 15:21	2	Prov. 15:21	1	48
326	17	19)	Prov. 15:23		Prov. 15:23		
327	13	15)	Prov. 15:25	1	Prov. 15:25	1	101
328	5	55)	Prov. 15:26		Prov. 15:26		
329	22	2)	Prov. 15:27	2	Prov. 15:27	1	150
330	5	56)	Prov. 15:29		Prov. 15:29		
331	17	20)	Prov. 15:31-33		Prov. 15:31-33		
332	7	19)	Prov. 16:3	1	Prov. 16:3	1	65
333	9	6)	Prov. 16:6	2	Prov. 16:6	2	76

NO.	LT	LOC #	CONDITIONAL PROMISES	C.P.	DOER OF THE WORD	CNDT	PG.
334	5	57)	Prov. 16:7	1	Prov. 16:7	1	49
335	7	20)	Prov. 16:13		Prov. 16:13		
336	18	10)	Prov. 16:17	2	Prov. 16:17	1	126
337	5	58)	Prov. 16:20		Prov. 16:20		
338	17	21)	Prov. 16:21-23		Prov. 16:21-23		
339	6	25)	Prov. 16:24	3	Prov. 16:24	1	58
340	10	3)	Prov. 16:31	1	Prov. 16:31	1	82
341	18	11)	Prov. 16:32		Prov. 16:32		
342	17	22)	Prov. 17:20	2	Prov. 17:20	1	120
343	6	26)	Prov. 17:22	1	Prov. 17:22	1	59
344	17	23)	Prov. 17:24	1	Prov. 17:24	1	120
345	12	28)	Prov. 18:10	2	Prov. 18:10	1	94
346	6	27)	Prov. 18:14	1	Prov. 18:14	1	59
347	5	59)	Prov. 18:16	2	Prov. 18:16	1	49
348	5	60)	Prov. 18:18		Prov. 18:18		
349	8	30)	Prov. 18:20	2	Prov. 18:20	2	71
350	6	28)	Prov. 18:21		Prov. 18:21		
351	5	61)	Prov. 18:22	3	Prov. 18:22	1	49
352	17	24)	Prov. 19:8		Prov. 19:8		
353	5	62)	Prov. 19:11		Prov. 19:11		
354	19	4)	Prov. 19:16	2	Prov. 19:16	1	132
355	3	7)	Prov. 19:17	3	Prov. 19:17	1	37
356	18	12)	Prov. 19:20	1	Prov. 19:20	2	126
357	5	63)	Prov. 19:23		Prov. 19:23		
358	2	9)	Prov. 20:7	1	Prov. 20:7	1	32
359	18	13)	Prov. 20:11	1	Prov. 20:11	1	126
360	8	31)	Prov. 20:13	1	Prov. 20:13	1	71
361	17	25)	Prov. 20:15	2	Prov. 20:15	1	120

NO.	LT	LOC #	CONDITIONAL PROMISES	C.P.	DOER OF THE WORD	CNDT	PG.
362	10	4)	Prov. 20:29	1	Prov. 20:29	1	82
363	18	14)	Prov. 20:29	1	Prov. 20:29	1	127
364	5	64)	Prov. 21:3		Prov. 21:3		
365	8	32)	Prov. 21:5	2	Prov. 21:5	1	71
366	17	26)	Prov. 21:11	1	Prov. 21:11	1	120
367	11	29)	Prov. 21:23	2	Prov. 21:23	2	87
368	5	65)	Prov. 22:4		Prov. 22:4		
369	8	33)	Prov. 22:4	1	Prov. 22:4	2	71
370	10	5)	Prov. 22:4	1	Prov. 22:4	2	82
371	6	50.4)	Prov. 22:5		Prov. 22:5		
372	2	10)	Prov. 22:6	1	Prov. 22:6	1	33
373	3	8)	Prov. 22:9	2	Prov. 22:9	2	37
374	5	66)	Prov. 22:11	2	Prov. 22:11	2	49
375	17	27)	Prov. 22:18-19		Prov. 22:17-18		
376	30	6)	Prov. 23:15-16	3	Prov. 23:15-16	2	196
377	19	5)	Prov. 23:18		Prov. 23:17		
378	8	34)	Prov. 24:3-4		Prov. 24:3-4		
379	5	67)	Prov. 24:25		Prov. 24:23, 25		
380	17	28)	Prov. 25:11-12		Prov. 25:11-12		
381	5	68)	Prov. 25:15		Prov. 25:15		
382	15	10)	Prov. 25:21-22		Prov. 25:21		
383	27	39.4)	Prov. 27:18		Prov. 27:18		
384	8	56.4)	Prov. 27:26-27		Prov. 27:23, 25		
385	17	29)	Prov. 28:2, 5		Prov. 28:2, 5		
386	15	11)	Prov. 28:10	1	Prov. 28:10	1	106
387	23	2)	Prov. 28:13	1	Prov. 28:13	2	154
388	6	29)	Prov. 28:14	1	Prov. 28:14	1	59
389	10	6)	Prov. 28:16	2	Prov. 28:16	1	83

NO.	LT	LOC #	CONDITIONAL PROMISES	C.P.	DOER OF THE WORD	CNDT	PG.
390	15	12)	Prov. 28:18	2	Prov. 28:18	1	106
391	8	57.4)	Prov. 28:19		Prov. 28:19		
392	7	21)	Prov. 28:20	1	Prov. 28:20	1	65
393	8	35)	Prov. 28:25	2	Prov. 28:25	1	71
394	15	13)	Prov. 28:26	2	Prov. 28:26	1	106
395	3	9)	Prov. 28:27	2	Prov. 28:27	1	37
396	7	22)	Prov. 29:2, 6, 14		Prov. 29:2, 6, 14		
397	2	11)	Prov. 29:15, 17		Prov. 29:15, 17		
398	18	15)	Prov. 29:16		Prov. 29:16		
399	5	69)	Prov. 29:18	1	Prov. 29:18	1	50
400	7	23)	Prov. 29:23	1	Prov. 29:23	1	65
401	11	30)	Prov. 29:25	2	Prov. 29:25	1	88
402	5	70)	Prov. 30:5	2	Prov. 30:5	1	50
403	2	12)	Prov. 31:30	2	Prov. 31:30	1	33
164	20	(164 C.P. found in 20 Life Topics)					
ECCLESIASTES							
404	17	30)	Eccl. 2:26		Eccl. 2:26		
405	6	30)	Eccl. 5:12	2	Eccl. 5:12	1	59
406	7	24)	Eccl. 7:8	1	Eccl. 7:8	1	65
407	6	31)	Eccl. 7:12		Eccl. 7:12		
408	10	7)	Eccl. 7:12	1	Eccl. 7:12	1	83
409	17	31)	Eccl. 7:12		Eccl. 7:12		
410	18	16)	Eccl. 7:12	1	Eccl. 7:12	1	127
411	18	17)	Eccl. 7:18		Eccl. 7:16-18		
412	17	32)	Eccl. 7:19	2	Eccl. 7:19	1	121
413	18	35.4)	Eccl. 7:26		Eccl. 7:26		
414	6	32)	Eccl. 8:1	2	Eccl. 8:1	1	59
415	5	71)	Eccl. 8:5		Eccl. 8:5		

NO.	LT	LOC #	CONDITIONAL PROMISES	C.P.	DOER OF THE WORD	CNDT	PG.
416	15	14)	Eccl. 8:12	1	Eccl. 8:12	2	107
417	17	33)	Eccl. 10:10, 12		Eccl. 10:10, 12		
418	8	58.4)	Eccl. 11:1		Eccl. 11:1		
419	3	29.4)	Eccl. 11:2		Eccl. 11:2		
420	18	18)	Eccl. 11:9		Eccl. 11:9-10		
17	9	(17 C.P. found in 9 Life Topics)					
		ISAIAH					
421	9	7)	Isa. 1:18		Isa. 1:16-18		
422	8	36)	Isa. 1:19	2	Isa. 1:19	2	72
423	19	64.4)	Isa. 8:14		Isa. 8:13, 17		
424	12	29)	Isa. 26:3-4	2	Isa. 26:3-4	3	94
425	27	40.4)	Isa. 28:5-6		Isa. 28:5-6		
426	11	47.4)	Isa. 28:16		Isa. 28:16		
427	9	8)	Isa. 29:24; 30:15		Isa. 29:23-24; 30:15		
428	5	72)	Isa. 30:18		Isa. 30:18		
429	9	28.4)	Isa. 30:19-21		Isa. 30:19, 22		
430	8	59.4)	Isa. 30:19, 23		Isa. 30:19, 22		
431	9	29.4)	Isa. 31:5		Isa. 31:6-7		
432	3	10)	Isa. 32:8	2	Isa. 32:8	1	37
433	3	30.4)	Isa. 32:17-18, 20		Isa. 32:17, 20		
434	5	73)	Isa. 33:6		Isa. 33:6		
435	11	48.4)	Isa. 33:15-16		Isa. 33:15		
436	15	50.4)	Isa. 35:4, 10		Isa. 35:3-4		
437	19	65.4)	Isa. 40:10-11		Isa. 40:9		
438	12	30)	Isa. 40:31	5	Isa. 40:31	1	94
439	12	31)	Isa. 41:10	4	Isa. 41:10	2	95
440	15	15)	Isa. 41:11		Isa. 41:13, 16		
441	11	31)	Isa. 41:12-13		Isa. 41:13, 16		

NO.	LT	LOC #	CONDITIONAL PROMISES	C.P.	DOER OF THE WORD	CNDT	PG.
442	12	58.4)	Isa. 43:1-2		Isa. 43:1		
443	23	3)	Isa. 43:25-26		Isa. 43:26		
444	2	13)	Isa. 44:3-5		Isa. 44:2, 8		
445	9	9)	Isa. 44:21-22		Isa. 44:22		
446	19	6)	Isa. 45:22, 25		Isa. 45:22, 25		
447	10	8)	Isa. 46:4	5	Isa. 46:3	I	83
448	9	10)	Isa. 46:13		Isa. 46:9, 12		
449	5	74)	Isa. 49:23	2	Isa. 49:23	I	50
450	19	66.4)	Isa. 51:3-4		Isa. 51:1-2, 4		
451	15	16)	Isa. 51:8		Isa. 51:7		
452	12	32)	Isa. 52:6		Isa. 52:1-2		
453	9	30.4)	Isa. 52:12		Isa. 52:11		
454	2	27.4)	Isa. 54:3, 13		Isa. 54:1-2, 4		
455	13	22.4)	Isa. 54:3-5, 8, 10		Isa. 54:1-2, 4		
456	12	59.4)	Isa. 54:14		Isa. 54:1-2, 4		
457	15	51.4)	Isa. 54:15	I	Isa. 54:1-2, 4	8	III
458	11	49.4)	Isa. 54:17		Isa. 54:1-2, 4		
459	9	11)	Isa. 55:7	2	Isa. 55:6-7	5	77
460	19	7)	Isa. 56:2, 5		Isa. 56:1		
461	5	75)	Isa. 57:1		Isa. 57:1		
462	22	3)	Isa. 57:1	I	Isa. 57:1	I	150
463	12	33)	Isa. 57:1-2	3	Isa. 57:1	I	95
464	5	151.4)	Isa. 57:13		Isa. 57:13		
465	8	60.4)	Isa. 57:13		Isa. 57:13		
466	31	6.4)	Isa. 57:13		Isa. 57:13		
467	9	12)	Isa. 57:15, 18-19		Isa. 57:15		
468	20	1)	Isa. 58:8-9		Isa. 58:6-7		
469	11	32)	Isa. 59:1, 19-20		Isa. 59:20		

NO.	LT	LOC #	CONDITIONAL PROMISES	C.P.	DOER OF THE WORD	CNDT	PG.
470	2	14)	Isa. 59:20-21		Isa. 59:20		
471	12	34)	Isa. 60:1-3		Isa. 60:1, 4		
472	5	152.4)	Isa. 61:1, 5-7		Isa. 61:1-3, 6		
473	19	67.4)	Isa. 62:1-3, 12		Isa. 62:10-11		
474	5	76)	Isa. 64:4-5		Isa. 64:4-5		
475	9	31.4)	Isa. 65:8, 13-14, 16		Isa. 65:16, 18		
476	5	77)	Isa. 66:2		Isa. 66:2		
477	27	41)	Isa. 66:11-14, 22, 24		Isa. 66:10		
57	17	(57 C.P. found in 17 Life Topics)					
		JEREMIAH					
478	18	19)	Jer. 1:8		Jer. 1:7, 8		
479	9	13)	Jer. 3:12, 14-15, 22; 4:1		Jer. 3:12-14, 19, 22; 4:1		
480	5	153.4)	Jer. 7:3, 5-7, 23		Jer. 7:3, 5-6, 23		
481	8	37)	Jer. 11:4-5		Jer. 11:4, 6-7		
482	21	3)	Jer. 12:16		Jer. 12:16		
483	7	54.4)	Jer. 15:19-21		Jer. 15:19		
484	15	17)	Jer. 17:7-8		Jer. 17:7		
485	5	78)	Jer. 17:10	2	Jer. 17:10	2	50
486	6	51.4)	Jer. 17:24-26		Jer. 17:21-22, 24		
487	5	79)	Jer. 18:7-8		Jer. 18:8, 11		
488	7	55.4)	Jer. 22:4		Jer. 22:3		
489	15	52.4)	Jer. 23: 3-4, 8		Jer. 23:7-8		
490	9	14)	Jer. 24:6-7		Jer. 24:7		
491	9	15)	Jer. 29:11-14		Jer. 29:12-13		
492	19	8)	Jer. 30:8, 10-11		Jer. 30:9-10		
493	6	33)	Jer. 30:17		Jer. 30:9-10		

NO.	LT	LOC #	CONDITIONAL PROMISES	C.P.	DOER OF THE WORD	CNDT	PG.
494	15	18)	Jer. 31:3-4, 8-9, 13-14		Jer. 31:7, 10, 14		
495	2	28.4)	Jer. 31:16-17		Jer. 31:16		
496	17	34)	Jer. 33:3	3	Jer. 33:3	1	121
497	9	16)	Jer. 35:15		Jer. 35:15		
498	12	60.4)	Jer. 42:10-11		Jer. 42:10-11, 19		
21	14	(21 C.P. found in 14 Life Topics)					
			LAMENTATIONS				
499	15	19)	Lam. 3:22-23, 25, 31-33		Lam. 3:24-26, 28, 40-41, 55		
1	1	(1 C.P. found in 1 Life Topics)					
			EZEKIEL				
500	25	1)	Ezek. 3:17, 19, 21		Ezek. 3:19, 21		
501	9	17)	Ezek. 11:17, 19-20		Ezek. 11:18		
502	23	4)	Ezek. 16:59-63		Ezek. 16:61, 63		
503	5	80)	Ezek. 18:4-9		Ezek. 18:5-9		
504	18	20)	Ezek. 18:14, 17, 19-20		Ezek. 18:14-17, 19-20		
505	9	18)	Ezek. 18:21-22, 27-28		Ezek. 18:21-22, 27-28, 31		
506	7	25)	Ezek. 33:9		Ezek. 33:9		
507	9	19)	Ezek. 33:14-16, 19		Ezek. 33:14-15, 19		
508	9	32.4)	Ezek. 37:21-23, 26-27		Ezek. 37:23-24		
9	6	(9 C.P. found in 6 Life Topics)					
			DANIEL				
509	5	81)	Dan. 9:4	3	Dan. 9:4	2	50
1	1	(1 C.P. found in 1 Life Topics)					

NO.	LT	LOC #	CONDITIONAL PROMISES	C.P.	DOER OF THE WORD	CNDT	PG.
			HOSEA				
510	9	33.4)	Hos. 14:4-7, 9		Hos. 14:1-2, 9		
1	1	(1 C.P. found in 1 Life Topics)					
			JOEL				
511	9	34.4)	Joel 2:13, 18-19, 23, 25-27		Joel 2:12-13, 15-17, 21, 23		
512	19	9)	Joel 2:28-29, 32		Joel 2:32		
2	2	(2 C.P. found in 2 Life Topics)					
			AMOS				
513	5	82)	Amos 5:14		Amos 5:14-15		
1	1	(1 C.P. found in 1 Life Topics)					
			MICAH				
514	5	83)	Mic. 2:7		Mic. 2:7		
515	9	35.4)	Mic. 2:12-13		Mic. 2:12-13		
516	21	58.4)	Mic. 4:1		Mic. 4:1-2		
517	8	61.4)	Mic. 4:13		Mic. 4:13		
518	11	33)	Mic. 7:7-9, 18-19		Mic. 6:8; 7:5, 7, 9		
5	5	(5 C.P. found in 5 Life Topics)					
			NAHUM				
519	11	34)	Nah. 1:7	3	Nah. 1:7	1	88
520	19	10)	Nah. 1:7	2	Nah. 1:7	1	132
2	2	(2 C.P. found in 2 Life Topics)					
			HABAKKUK				
521	5	84)	Hab. 3:19		Hab. 3:18		
1	1	(1 C.P. found in 1 Life Topics)					
			ZEPHANIAH				
522	21	4)	Zeph. 3:9, 11-13, 15, 17		Zeph. 3:9-14, 16		

NO.	LT	LOC #	CONDITIONAL PROMISES	C.P.	DOER OF THE WORD	CNDT	PG.
523	5	85)	Zeph. 3:19		Zeph. 3:14, 16		
524	6	34)	Zeph. 3:19		Zeph. 3:14, 16		
525	11	35)	Zeph. 3:19	1	Zeph. 3:14, 16	6	88
526	9	20)	Zeph. 3:13, 20		Zeph. 3:13-14, 16		
5	5	(5 C.P. found in 5 Life Topics)					

HAGGAI

NO.	LT	LOC #	CONDITIONAL PROMISES	C.P.	DOER OF THE WORD	CNDT	PG.
527	5	86)	Hag. 2:4-5		Hag. 2:4-5		
1	1	(1 C.P. found in 1 Life Topics)					

ZECHARIAH

NO.	LT	LOC #	CONDITIONAL PROMISES	C.P.	DOER OF THE WORD	CNDT	PG.
528	9	21)	Zech. 1:3	1	Zech. 1:3-4	2	77
529	19	11)	Zech. 2:10	2	Zech. 2:10	1	132
530	5	87)	Zech. 3:7		Zech. 3:7		
531	19	12)	Zech. 8:3, 7-8, 12-13		Zech. 8:9, 13, 15-17, 19		
532	15	20)	Zech. 9:11-12, 15-17; 10:1, 3, 5-8, 12		Zech. 10:1, 7, 9, 12		
533	15	21)	Zech. 13:8-9		Zech. 13:9		
6	4	(6 C.P. found in 4 Life Topics)					

MALACHI

NO.	LT	LOC #	CONDITIONAL PROMISES	C.P.	DOER OF THE WORD	CNDT	PG.
534	5	88)	Mal. 1:9		Mal. 1:9		
535	9	22)	Mal. 3:6-7	2	Mal. 3:7	1	77
536	3	11)	Mal. 3:10-12	4	Mal. 3:10	2	38
537	19	13)	Mal. 4:2-3		Mal. 4:2-4		
4	4	(4 C.P. found in 4 Life Topics)					

MATTHEW

NO.	LT	LOC #	CONDITIONAL PROMISES	C.P.	DOER OF THE WORD	CNDT	PG.
538	23	5)	Matt. 4:17	1	Matt. 4:17	1	154
539	21	5)	Matt. 4:19	1	Matt. 4:19	1	142

NO.	LT	LOC #	CONDITIONAL PROMISES	C.P.	DOER OF THE WORD	CNDT	PG.
540	5	154.4)	Matt. 5:3		Matt. 5:3		
541	24	12.4)	Matt. 5:4		Matt. 5:4		
542	8	62.4)	Matt. 5:5		Matt. 5:5		
543	5	155.4)	Matt. 5:6		Matt. 5:6		
544	5	89)	Matt. 5:7	2	Matt. 5:7	1	51
545	30	7)	Matt. 5:8	2	Matt. 5:8	1	196
546	5	90)	Matt. 5:9	2	Matt. 5:9	1	51
547	15	22)	Matt. 5:10-11		Matt. 5:10, 12		
548	5	91)	Matt. 5:16	2	Matt. 5:16	1	51
549	19	14)	Matt. 5:19	2	Matt. 5:19	2	133
550	3	12)	Matt. 5:23, 25-26		Matt. 5:23-25		
551	21	6)	Matt. 5:23, 25-26		Matt. 5:23-25		
552	26	1)	Matt. 5:23, 25-26		Matt. 5:23-25		
553	5	92)	Matt. 5:45		Matt. 5:44, 48		
554	3	13)	Matt. 6:4	1	Matt. 6:1-4	4	39
555	24	2)	Matt. 6:6	2	Matt. 6:6-7	2	158
556	5	93)	Matt. 6:14	2	Matt. 6:14	1	51
557	20	2)	Matt. 6:17-18	2	Matt. 6:17-18	3	138
558	3	14)	Matt. 6:21	1	Matt. 6:20	1	39
559	6	35)	Matt. 6:22	2	Matt. 6:22	1	60
560	8	38)	Matt. 6:32-34		Matt. 6:25, 31, 33-34		
561	5	94)	Matt. 7:1, 5		Matt. 7:1, 5		
562	17	35)	Matt. 7:7-8		Matt. 7:7-8		
563	5	95)	Matt. 7:12	1	Matt. 7:12	1	51
564	18	36.4)	Matt. 7:16, 20		Matt. 7:15		

NO.	LT	LOC #	CONDITIONAL PROMISES	C.P.	DOER OF THE WORD	CNDT	PG.
565	17	36)	Matt. 7:24		Matt. 7:24		
566	20	3.4)	Matt. 9:15		Matt. 9:15		
567	25	2)	Matt. 9:37		Matt. 9:38		
568	26	32.4)	Matt. 10:19-20, 22, 26, 32		Matt. 10:6-8, 12-13, 16-17, 19, 22, 26-28, 31-32		
569	15	23)	Matt. 10:39	2	Matt. 10:39	1	107
570	21	7)	Matt. 10:40	2	Matt. 10:40	1	142
571	28	1)	Matt. 10:41-42		Matt. 10:41-42		
572	30	8)	Matt. 11:6	1	Matt. 11:6	1	197
573	6	36)	Matt. 11:28-30		Matt. 11:28-29		
574	17	37)	Matt. 12:35, 37	2	Matt. 12:35, 37	2	121
575	17	38)	Matt. 13:12		Matt. 13:12		
576	19	15)	Matt. 13:43	1	Matt. 13:43	1	133
577	24	3)	Matt. 15:28		Matt. 15:28		
578	24	4)	Matt. 16:19	3	Matt. 16:19	2	158
579	15	24)	Matt. 16:25	2	Matt. 16:25	1	107
580	27	2)	Matt. 16:27	1	Matt. 16:27	1	178
581	24	5)	Matt. 17:20	3	Matt. 17:20	1	158
582	21	8)	Matt. 18:3-5		Matt. 18:3-5		
583	22	25.4)	Matt. 18:8-9		Matt. 18:8-9		
584	2	15)	Matt. 18:10, 14		Matt. 18:10		
585	26	2)	Matt. 18:15-17		Matt. 18:15-17		
586	24	6)	Matt. 18:18-20	8	Matt. 18:18-20	4	159
587	26	3)	Matt. 18:35		Matt. 18:35		
588	2	16)	Matt. 19:5-6		Matt. 19:5-6		
589	2	17)	Matt. 19:14		Matt. 19:14		

NO.	LT	LOC #	CONDITIONAL PROMISES	C.P.	DOER OF THE WORD	CNDT	PG.
590	21	9)	Matt. 19:17, 21		Matt. 19:17-19, 21		
591	8	39)	Matt. 19:29		Matt. 19:29		
592	21	10)	Matt. 19:29	3	Matt. 19:29	8	142
593	15	25)	Matt. 19:30; 20:16		Matt. 19:30; 20:16		
594	24	7)	Matt. 21:21-22	4	Matt. 21:21-22	4	159
595	31	1)	Matt. 21:43	1	Matt. 21:43	1	202
596	7	26)	Matt. 23:12		Matt. 23:8-10, 12		
597	18	21)	Matt. 23:12	2	Matt. 23:12	1	127
598	27	3)	Matt. 24:13	2	Matt. 24:4, 13	2	178
599	27	4)	Matt. 24:46-47	2	Matt. 24:46	1	178
600	8	63.4)	Matt. 25:21, 23, 29		Matt. 25:21, 23		
601	27	5)	Matt. 25:34		Matt. 25:35-36		
602	27	6)	Matt. 26:29		Matt. 26:26-27		
603	22	4)	Matt. 26:41	1	Matt. 26:41	2	150
604	7	56.4)	Matt. 26:52		Matt. 26:52		
605	25	3)	Matt. 28:20	1	Matt. 28:19-20	5	168
69	21	(69 C.P. found in 21 Life Topics)					

MARK

NO.	LT	LOC #	CONDITIONAL PROMISES	C.P.	DOER OF THE WORD	CNDT	PG.
606	21	11)	Mark 1:15, 17		Mark 1:15, 17		
607	28	2)	Mark 1:17		Mark 1:17		
608	21	12)	Mark 2:17	1	Mark 2:17	1	142
609	19	16)	Mark 2:27	1	Mark 2:27	1	133
610	5	96)	Mark 3:35	2	Mark 3:35	1	52
611	17	39)	Mark 4:9, 11, 20		Mark 4:9, 20		

NO.	LT	LOC #	CONDITIONAL PROMISES	C.P.	DOER OF THE WORD	CNDT	PG.
612	22	5)	Mark 4:22-23		Mark 4:23-24		
613	17	40)	Mark 4:24-25		Mark 4:24-25		
614	18	22)	Mark 7:15-16		Mark 7:14, 16		
615	21	13)	Mark 8:34-35		Mark 8:34-35		
616	11	36)	Mark 9:23	2	Mark 9:23	1	88
617	29	1)	Mark 9:29	1	Mark 9:29	2	192
618	21	14)	Mark 9:37		Mark 9:37		
619	29	2)	Mark 9:39-40	4	Mark 9:39-40	3	192
620	19	17)	Mark 9:41		Mark 9:41		
621	5	97)	Mark 9:49		Mark 9:50		
622	2	18)	Mark 10:6, 8-9		Mark 10:7, 9		
623	21	15)	Mark 10:14-15		Mark 10:15		
624	3	15)	Mark 10:21		Mark 10:21		
625	8	40)	Mark 10:23-24, 27		Mark 10:23-24, 27		
626	3	16)	Mark 10:29-31		Mark 10:29, 31		
627	21	16)	Mark 10:29-31		Mark 10:29, 31		
628	7	27)	Mark 10:42-45		Mark 10:43		
629	24	8)	Mark 11:23-25		Mark 11:22-25		
630	27	7)	Mark 13:13	2	Mark 13:13, 33, 37	5	178
631	25	4)	Mark 16:16-18	8	Mark 16:15-17	4	169
26	14	(26 C.P. found in 14 Life Topics)					
			LUKE				
632	25	5)	Luke 5:10	1	Luke 5:10	1	169
633	20	4.4)	Luke 5:35		Luke 5:35		
634	13	23.4)	Luke 6:20-21		Luke 6:20-21		
635	12	35)	Luke 6:21		Luke 6:21		

NO.	LT	LOC #	CONDITIONAL PROMISES	C.P.	DOER OF THE WORD	CNDT	PG.
636	15	26)	Luke 6:22-23	5	Luke 6:23	2	107
637	5	98)	Luke 6:27, 35, 37-38		Luke 6:27, 35, 37-38		
638	3	17)	Luke 6:38	5	Luke 6:38	2	40
639	7	28)	Luke 6:40	2	Luke 6:40	1	65
640	26	4)	Luke 6:42	1	Luke 6:42	1	174
641	17	41)	Luke 6:47-48		Luke 6:47-48		
642	21	17)	Luke 7:23	1	Luke 7:23	1	143
643	12	36)	Luke 8:8, 10, 15		Luke 8:8, 15		
644	23	6)	Luke 8:17-18	4	Luke 8:18	2	154
645	19	18)	Luke 8:21	2	Luke 8:21	2	133
646	6	52.4)	Luke 8:48, 50		Luke 8:48, 50, 52		
647	28	3)	Luke 9:23-24	3	Luke 9:23-24	5	186
648	7	29)	Luke 9:48		Luke 9:48		
649	26	5)	Luke 9:50		Luke 9:50		
650	28	4)	Luke 9:62		Luke 9:59, 60		
651	25	6)	Luke 10:7, 11, 16		Luke 10:2-3, 9		
652	17	42)	Luke 10:23		Luke 10:23		
653	5	99)	Luke 10:27, 28		Luke 10:27		
654	24	9)	Luke 11:9-10, 13	10	Luke 11:9-10, 13	7	160
655	18	23)	Luke 11:28	1	Luke 11:28	2	127
656	6	37)	Luke 11:34, 36		Luke 11:35, 36		
657	3	18)	Luke 11:41	1	Luke 11:41	1	40
658	5	156.4)	Luke 12:1-3		Luke 12:1		
659	11	37)	Luke 12:5, 7		Luke 12:4-5, 7		
660	21	18)	Luke 12:8	2	Luke 12:8	1	143

NO.	LT	LOC #	CONDITIONAL PROMISES	C.P.	DOER OF THE WORD	CNDT	PG.
661	15	27)	Luke 12:11-12		Luke 12:11		
662	8	41)	Luke 12:15, 30-33		Luke 12:15, 22, 24, 27, 29, 31-33		
663	27	8)	Luke 12:35-38, 40, 43, 48		Luke 12:35-38, 40, 43, 48		
664	23	13.4)	Luke 13:3, 5		Luke 13:3, 5		
665	21	59.4)	Luke 13:30		Luke 13:24		
666	5	100)	Luke 14:11	2	Luke 14:11	1	52
667	3	19)	Luke 14:14		Luke 14:13		
668	27	9)	Luke 14:14	2	Luke 14:13	4	179
669	15	28)	Luke 14:26-27		Luke 14:26-27		
670	21	19)	Luke 15:7, 10		Luke 15:7		
671	9	23)	Luke 15:7, 10	3	Luke 15:7, 10	2	78
672	23	7)	Luke 15:7, 10	3	Luke 15:7, 10	2	155
673	8	42)	Luke 16:10	2	Luke 16:10	1	72
674	26	6)	Luke 17:1, 3-4		Luke 17:3-4		
675	24	20.4)	Luke 17:6		Luke 17:6		
676	28	5)	Luke 17:20-21, 33	4	Luke 17:33	1	186
677	24	10)	Luke 18:7-8		Luke 18:7		
678	18	24)	Luke 18:14, 16-17		Luke 18:14, 16-17		
679	5	101)	Luke 18:22		Luke 18:20, 22		
680	3	20)	Luke 18:29-30		Luke 18:29-30		
681	8	43)	Luke 18:29-30		Luke 18:29		
682	5	102)	Luke 20:18		Luke 20:18		
683	21	20)	Luke 20:18		Luke 20:18		
684	27	10)	Luke 20:35-36		Luke 20:35		

NO.	LT	LOC #	CONDITIONAL PROMISES	C.P.	DOER OF THE WORD	CNDT	PG.
685	15	29)	Luke 21:34, 36		Luke 21:34, 36		
686	7	30)	Luke 22:26, 28-30		Luke 22:26, 28		
687	22	26.4)	Luke 22:40, 46		Luke 22:40, 46		
56	23	(56 C.P. found in 23 Life Topics)					

JOHN

NO.	LT	LOC #	CONDITIONAL PROMISES	C.P.	DOER OF THE WORD	CNDT	PG.
688	21	21)	John 1:12-13	4	John 1:12-13	3	143
689	21	22)	John 3:3, 5, 15-16, 18, 21, 36		John 3:3, 5, 7, 15-16, 18, 21, 36		
690	21	60.4)	John 4:14		John 4:14		
691	5	103)	John 4:23-24		John 4:23-24		
692	25	25.4)	John 4:35-37		John 4:35-36		
693	21	23)	John 5:24	4	John 5:24	2	143
694	27	11)	John 5:25	2	John 5:25	1	179
695	16	5)	John 5:28-29		John 5:28		
696	19	19)	John 6:35, 37, 40		John 6:35, 37, 40		
697	21	24)	John 6:47	2	John 6:47	1	144
698	21	61.4)	John 6:51, 53-57		John 6:51, 53-57		
699	17	43)	John 7:17		John 7:17		
700	21	25)	John 7:37-38		John 7:37-38		
701	21	26)	John 8:12	3	John 8:12	1	144
702	30	9)	John 8:31-32	4	John 8:31	1	197
703	17	44)	John 8:47	2	John 8:47	1	121
704	21	27)	John 8:47		John 8:47		
705	16	6)	John 8:51	2	John 8:51	1	115
706	5	104)	John 9:31	2	John 9:31	2	52
707	7	57.4)	John 10:2		John 10:2, 4		

NO.	LT	LOC #	CONDITIONAL PROMISES	C.P.	DOER OF THE WORD	CNDT	PG.
708	21	62.4)	John 10:9		John 10:9		
709	19	20)	John 10:27-29		John 10:27		
710	17	62.4)	John 11:9		John 11:9		
711	21	28)	John 11:25-26	4	John 11:25-26	3	144
712	5	105)	John 12:25-26		John 12:25-26		
713	25	7)	John 12:32, 36	4	John 12:32, 35-36	3	170
714	5	106)	John 12:44-46		John 12:44-46		
715	7	58.4)	John 13:10, 14-15, 17		John 13:10, 14-15, 17		
716	5	107)	John 13:20		John 13:20		
717	26	7)	John 13:34-35	2	John 13:34-35	4	174
718	27	12)	John 14:2-3	2	John 14:1	3	179
719	21	29)	John 14:6-7, 9	6	John 14:7, 9, 11	4	145
720	28	6)	John 14:12	3	John 14:12	1	186
721	24	21.4)	John 14:13-14	5	John 14:13-14	2	164
722	5	108	John 14:15-21, 23		John 14:15, 21, 23		
723	17	45)	John 14:26-27		John 14:27		
724	19	68.4)	John 15:1-5		John 15:2, 4-5		
725	21	63.4)	John 15:1-5		John 15:2, 4-5		
726	24	11)	John 15:7	3	John 15:7	3	160
727	5	109)	John 15:8		John 15:8		
728	18	25)	John 15:8		John 15:8		
729	30	10)	John 15:9-15		John 15:9-10, 12-14		
730	5	110)	John 15:16-17		John 15:16-17		
731	15	30)	John 15:18-20; 16:1, 4		John 15:18		

NO.	LT	LOC #	CONDITIONAL PROMISES	C.P.	DOER OF THE WORD	CNDT	PG.
732	24	22.4)	John 16:23-27	8	John 16:23-24, 26-27	5	165
733	12	37)	John 16:33		John 16:33		
734	15	31)	John 16:33	2	John 16:33	1	108
735	24	12)	John 20:21, 23		John 20:22, 23		
736	21	30)	John 20:29		John 20:29		
49	15	(49 C.P. found in 15 Life Topics)					
ACTS							
737	31	2)	Acts 1:5, 8	3	Acts 1:8	4	202
738	21	31)	Acts 2:21	2	Acts 2:21	1	145
739	31	3)	Acts 2:38-39	5	Acts 2:38	2	203
740	5	111)	Acts 2:47		Acts 2:46-47		
741	21	32)	Acts 3:19-21		Acts 3:19		
742	21	33)	Acts 4:10, 12	2	Acts 4:12	1	145
743	25	8)	Acts 5:32		Acts 5:32		
744	17	63.4)	Acts 5:38-39		Acts 5:35, 38		
745	6	53.4)	Acts 10:15		Acts 10:15		
746	21	34)	Acts 10:34-35		Acts 10:35		
747	6	38)	Acts 11:9		Acts 11:9		
748	19	21)	Acts 13:38-39		Acts 13:39		
749	6	54.4)	Acts 14:10		Acts 14:9		
750	21	35)	Acts 16:31	2	Acts 16:31	1	146
751	27	13)	Acts 17:27-28, 30		Acts 17:27, 30		
752	25	26.4)	Acts 18:10		Acts 18:9		
753	28	7)	Acts 20:24		Acts 20:24		
754	3	21)	Acts 20:32, 35		Acts 20:28, 32, 35		
755	7	31)	Acts 20:32, 35		Acts 20:28, 32, 35		

NO.	LT	LOC #	CONDITIONAL PROMISES	C.P.	DOER OF THE WORD	CNDT	PG.
756	25	27.4)	Acts 26:16-18		Acts 26:16, 18		
20	11	(20 C.P. found in 11 Life Topics)					
			ROMANS				
757	5	112)	Rom. 1:6-7		Rom. 1:5		
758	19	22)	Rom. 1:16-17		Rom. 1:16-17		
759	5	113)	Rom. 2:1		Rom. 2:1		
760	23	8)	Rom. 2:2, 4, 6-7, 10-11		Rom. 2:7, 10		
761	19	23)	Rom. 2:28-29		Rom. 2:29		
762	21	36)	Rom. 3:22, 26, 28		Rom. 3:22, 26, 28		
763	32	1)	Rom. 3:28; 4:5, 16	5	Rom. 3:28; 4:5, 12, 16	5	206
764	19	24)	Rom. 4:22-24		Rom. 4:20-21, 24		
765	12	38)	Rom. 5:1-5		Rom. 5:1-4		
766	19	25)	Rom. 5:10-11		Rom. 5:11		
767	32	2)	Rom. 5:17, 20-21	4	Rom. 5:17	2	207
768	32	3)	Rom. 6:7-9, 12, 14, 23		Rom. 6:7-9, 11-13		
769	32	4)	Rom. 7:4, 6		Rom. 7:4, 6		
770	32	5)	Rom. 8:1-4		Rom. 8:1, 4		
771	6	39)	Rom. 8:6	2	Rom. 8:6	1	60
772	31	4)	Rom. 8:9-11, 13		Rom. 8:9-11, 13		
773	19	26)	Rom. 8:14, 16		Rom. 8:14-15		
774	15	32)	Rom. 8:16-18		Rom. 8:17-18		
775	11	38)	Rom. 8:28	3	Rom. 8:28	2	89
776	12	39)	Rom. 8:28	3	Rom. 8:28	2	95

NO.	LT	LOC #	CONDITIONAL PROMISES	C.P.	DOER OF THE WORD	CNDT	PG.
777	13	16)	Rom. 8:28	3	Rom. 8:28	2	101
778	15	33)	Rom. 8:28	3	Rom. 8:28	2	108
779	18	26)	Rom. 8:28	3	Rom. 8:28	2	127
780	21	37)	Rom. 8:28		Rom. 8:28		
781	14	2)	Rom. 8:38-39		Rom. 8:38-39		
782	16	7)	Rom. 8:38-39	3	Rom. 8:38	1	115
783	15	34)	Rom. 8:38-39	3	Rom. 8:38	1	108
784	29	3)	Rom. 8:38-39	3	Rom. 8:38	1	192
785	1	4)	Rom. 8:39		Rom. 8:38		
786	32	6)	Rom. 10:4	1	Rom. 10:4	1	202
787	21	38)	Rom. 10:4, 8-13		Rom. 10:4, 9-13		
788	25	9)	Rom. 10:15	2	Rom. 10:15	2	170
789	33	1)	Rom. 10:17	2	Rom. 10:17	1	212
790	19	69.4)	Rom. 11:18, 22-23		Rom. 11:18, 20, 22-23		
791	28	8)	Rom. 12:2	3	Rom. 12:1-2	5	187
792	33	2)	Rom. 12:3-8		Rom. 12:3, 6-8		
793	5	114)	Rom. 12:19-20		Rom. 12:18-21		
794	5	115)	Rom. 13:3		Rom. 13:1, 3, 5		
795	8	64.4)	Rom. 13:5-6		Rom. 13:5-7		
796	32	7)	Rom. 13:8, 10	3	Rom. 13:8-10	9	208
797	5	116)	Rom. 13:8-10		Rom. 13:8-10		
798	22	6)	Rom. 13:11-12		Rom. 13:11-14		
799	26	8)	Rom. 14:3-4, 12, 14, 17-18, 20, 22-23		Rom. 14:1, 3, 13-14, 16, 18-22		
800	19	27)	Rom. 15:4, 6		Rom. 15:1-2, 5		
801	5	117)	Rom. 15:7		Rom. 15:7		
802	26	9)	Rom. 15:7	1	Rom. 15:7	1	174

NO.	LT	LOC #	CONDITIONAL PROMISES	C.P.	DOER OF THE WORD	CNDT	PG.
803	12	40)	Rom. 15:13; 16:20		Rom. 15:13; 16:16-17, 19		
47	23	(47 C.P. found in 23 Life Topics)					

<table>

I CORINTHIANS

NO.	LT	LOC #	CONDITIONAL PROMISES	C.P.	DOER OF THE WORD	CNDT	PG.
804	19	28)	I Cor. 1:2-3		I Cor. 1:2		
805	33	3)	I Cor. 1:7-8		I Cor. 1:7		
806	27	14)	I Cor. 1:8	2	I Cor. 1:7	I	108
807	26	10)	I Cor. 1:9		I Cor. 1:10		
808	21	39)	I Cor. 1:18, 21		I Cor. 1:18, 21		
809	5	118)	I Cor. 1:27-31		I Cor. 1:29, 31		
810	17	46)	I Cor. 1:27-31		I Cor. 1:29, 31		
811	17	47)	I Cor. 2:9	3	I Cor. 2:9	I	121
812	28	9)	I Cor. 2:10-12		I Cor. 2:13		
813	17	48)	I Cor. 2:14-16		I Cor. 2:14-15		
814	28	10)	I Cor. 3:8-9		I Cor. 3:8-10		
815	27	15)	I Cor. 3:13-15		I Cor. 3:14-15		
816	22	27.4)	I Cor. 3:16-17		I Cor. 3:17		
817	17	49)	I Cor. 3:18		I Cor. 3:18		
818	5	119)	I Cor. 3:21, 23		I Cor. 3:21		
819	7	32)	I Cor. 4:2		I Cor. 4:2		
820	27	16)	I Cor. 4:4-5		I Cor. 4:3-5		
821	26	11)	I Cor. 4:20		I Cor. 4:6		
822	26	12)	I Cor. 5:5		I Cor. 5:4-5		
823	23	28.4)	I Cor. 5:6-7		I Cor. 5:7-8		
824	27	13)	I Cor. 5:13		I Cor. 5:11, 13		
825	16	8)	I Cor. 6:14, 17		I Cor. 6:17		
826	22	7)	I Cor. 6:19-20	5	I Cor. 6:20	2	150
827	2	19)	I Cor. 7:14-15		I Cor. 7:10-11, 15		

NO.	LT	LOC #	CONDITIONAL PROMISES	C.P.	DOER OF THE WORD	CNDT	PG.
828	5	157.4)	1 Cor. 7:22		1 Cor. 7:17, 20, 23-24		
829	27	17)	1 Cor. 7:26, 28-29, 31		1 Cor. 7:26-31		
830	17	50)	1 Cor. 8:1		1 Cor. 8:1		
831	30	11)	1 Cor. 8:3-4, 6		1 Cor. 8:3, 6		
832	26	33.4)	1 Cor. 8:8-9, 12		1 Cor. 8:8-9, 12-13		
833	7	33)	1 Cor. 9:14, 17		1 Cor. 9:14, 17		
834	25	10)	1 Cor. 9:19-23		1 Cor. 9:19-23		
835	22	8)	1 Cor. 9:27		1 Cor. 9:26-27		
836	17	51)	1 Cor. 10:6, 11-12		1 Cor. 10:6-10, 12		
837	22	29.4)	1 Cor. 10:13		1 Cor. 10:14		
838	25	11)	1 Cor. 10:23, 26, 28-29, 33		1 Cor. 10:24-25, 27-28, 31-33; 11:1		
839	27	18)	1 Cor. 11:26, 31-32		1 Cor. 11:26, 28, 31, 33		
840	33	4)	1 Cor. 12:3	4	1 Cor. 12:3	2	212
841	26	14)	1 Cor. 12:24, 26-27		1 Cor. 12:25-26		
842	5	120)	1 Cor. 12:31; 13:8, 13		1 Cor. 13:4-7; 14:1		
843	33	5)	1 Cor. 14:2-5		1 Cor. 14:1-5, 13		
844	33	6)	1 Cor. 14:33	2	1 Cor. 14:26, 33, 40	3	212
845	27	19)	1 Cor. 15:22-24	5	1 Cor. 15:22-23	2	180
846	22	9)	1 Cor. 15:33-34	2	1 Cor. 15:33-34	3	151
847	16	9)	1 Cor. 15:58		1 Cor. 15:58		

NO.	LT	LOC #	CONDITIONAL PROMISES	C.P.	DOER OF THE WORD	CNDT	PG.
848	15	35)	1 Cor. 16:22		1 Cor. 16:13-14, 22		
45	15	(45 C.P. found in 15 Life Topics)					
			2 CORINTHIANS				
849	15	36)	2 Cor. 1:3-4, 7	5	2 Cor. 1:4, 7	2	109
850	16	10)	2 Cor. 1:9-10		2 Cor. 1:10		
851	19	29)	2 Cor. 1:20-22		2 Cor. 1:24		
852	26	15)	2 Cor. 2:11		2 Cor. 2:4-5, 7-11		
853	5	121)	2 Cor. 2:14-16		2 Cor. 2:14, 17		
854	32	15.4)	2 Cor. 3:3, 6		2 Cor. 3:4-5		
855	19	30)	2 Cor. 3:14, 16-18		2 Cor. 3:16		
856	25	12)	2 Cor. 4:6-7		2 Cor. 4:2, 5		
857	11	39)	2 Cor. 4:10-11, 14-18		2 Cor. 4:8-10, 14-16, 18		
858	19	31)	2 Cor. 5:1, 3-5		2 Cor. 5:1-4, 6-8		
859	27	20)	2 Cor. 5:10-11		2 Cor. 5:9, 11		
860	19	32)	2 Cor. 5:14-15, 17		2 Cor. 5:14-17		
861	28	11)	2 Cor. 5:18-19, 21		2 Cor. 5:18-20		
862	25	13)	2 Cor. 6:1-2		2 Cor. 6:1-2		
863	7	34)	2 Cor. 6:3		2 Cor. 6:3-10		
864	13	17)	2 Cor. 6:16-18		2 Cor. 6:14, 17; 7:1		
865	21	40)	2 Cor. 7:10		2 Cor. 7:10		
866	3	22)	2 Cor. 8:12, 14		2 Cor. 8:12		
867	3	23)	2 Cor. 9:6-8		2 Cor. 9:6-7		
868	29	4)	2 Cor. 10:3-4, 6	3	2 Cor. 10:3-6	6	193

NO.	LT	LOC #	CONDITIONAL PROMISES	C.P.	DOER OF THE WORD	CNDT	PG.
869	30	12)	2 Cor. 10:18	1	2 Cor. 10:17	1	197
870	12	41)	2 Cor. 12:9-10		2 Cor. 12:9-10		
871	28	12)	2 Cor. 12:12, 15		2 Cor. 12:12, 14-15, 19, 21		
872	19	33)	2 Cor. 13:5	2	2 Cor. 13:5	1	134
873	26	16)	2 Cor. 13:11		2 Cor. 13:11-12		
25	17	(25 C.P. found in 17 Life Topics)					

GALATIANS

NO.	LT	LOC #	CONDITIONAL PROMISES	C.P.	DOER OF THE WORD	CNDT	PG.
874	19	34)	Gal. 2:16, 20-21		Gal. 2:16, 20-21		
875	19	35)	Gal. 3:6-9		Gal. 3:6-7, 9		
876	32	8)	Gal. 3:11-14	4	Gal. 3:11, 14	2	208
877	21	41)	Gal. 3:22		Gal. 3:22		
878	32	9)	Gal. 3:24-25	2	Gal. 3:24	1	209
879	19	36)	Gal. 3:26-29		Gal. 3:26-27, 29		
880	32	10)	Gal. 4:28, 31; 5:6		Gal. 5:1, 5-6		
881	26	17)	Gal. 5:8-9, 14		Gal. 5:10, 13-14		
882	22	10)	Gal. 5:16, 24-25		Gal. 5:16, 24-26		
883	32	11)	Gal. 5:18-19, 22-23	5	Gal. 5:18, 22-23	10	209
884	26	18)	Gal. 6:2-4		Gal. 6:2, 4-5		
885	3	24)	Gal. 6:7-9		Gal. 6:6-10		
886	12	42)	Gal. 6:15-16		Gal. 6:15-16		
13	7	(13 C.P. found in 7 Life Topics)					

EPHESIANS

NO.	LT	LOC #	CONDITIONAL PROMISES	C.P.	DOER OF THE WORD	CNDT	PG.
887	19	37)	Eph. 1:3-14		Eph. 1:12-13		
888	17	52)	Eph. 1:17-19		Eph. 1:19		
889	21	42)	Eph. 2:8-10		Eph. 2:8, 10		

NO.	LT	LOC #	CONDITIONAL PROMISES	C.P.	DOER OF THE WORD	CNDT	PG.
890	25	14)	Eph. 3:6, 9-12		Eph. 3:2, 9-10, 12		
891	7	35)	Eph. 4:4-6		Eph. 4:1-3		
892	7	36)	Eph. 4:7, 12, 15-16		Eph. 4:11, 14-15		
893	19	38)	Eph. 4:21, 24		Eph. 4:21-24		
894	9	36.4)	Eph. 5:13-14		Eph. 5:14		
895	21	64.4)	Eph. 5:13-14		Eph. 5:14		
896	25	28.4)	Eph. 5:13-14		Eph. 5:14		
897	5	122)	Eph. 5:16		Eph. 5:15-21		
898	2	29.4)	Eph. 5:26-28, 31		Eph. 5:25, 28, 31		
899	10	9)	Eph. 6:1, 3	3	Eph. 6:2	2	83
900	18	27)	Eph. 6:1, 3	3	Eph. 6:1-2	3	128
901	5	123)	Eph. 6:8		Eph. 6:5-8		
902	7	37)	Eph. 6:9		Eph. 6:9		
903	29	5)	Eph. 6:10-13		Eph. 6:10-11, 13-18		
904	12	43)	Eph. 6:23-24		Eph. 6:24		
18	13	(18 C.P. found in 13 Life Topics)					
PHILIPPIANS							
905	31	5)	Phil. 1:6	1	Phil. 1:6	1	203
906	16	11)	Phil. 1:19-21		Phil. 1:19-20, 25		
907	15	37)	Phil. 1:28-29		Phil. 1:27-28		
908	33	7)	Phil. 2:13	2	Phil. 2:12	2	213
909	5	124)	Phil. 2:15		Phil. 2:14, 16		
910	19	39)	Phil. 3:3		Phil. 3:1-3		
911	32	16.4)	Phil. 3:3		Phil. 3:1-3		

NO.	LT	LOC #	CONDITIONAL PROMISES	C.P.	DOER OF THE WORD	CNDT	PG.
912	21	43)	Phil. 3:8-9		Phil. 3:7-9		
913	32	12)	Phil. 3:8-9		Phil. 3:7-9		
914	33	8)	Phil. 3:12, 15		Phil. 3:12-16		
915	27	21)	Phil. 3:20-21	4	Phil. 3:20; 4:1	2	181
916	5	125)	Phil. 4:5		Phil. 4:4-5		
917	24	13)	Phil. 4:7	2	Phil. 4:6	4	161
918	12	44)	Phil. 4:9	1	Phil. 4:8-9	13	96
919	8	44)	Phil. 4:13		Phil. 4:11-12		
920	3	25)	Phil. 4:18-19		Phil. 4:14-18		
16	13	(16 C.P. found in 13 Life Topics)					
		COLOSSIANS					
921	17	53)	Col. 1:9-11		Col. 1:4, 8, 12		
922	19	40)	Col. 1:12, 21-23		Col. 1:23		
923	28	13)	Col. 1:25, 27-28		Col. 1:25, 28		
924	17	54)	Col. 2:2		Col. 2:6-7		
925	5	126)	Col. 2:8-10		Col. 2:8		
926	6	40)	Col. 2:21-23		Col. 2:16, 18; 3:1-2		
927	5	127)	Col. 3:4, 10-11		Col. 3:5, 8-10		
928	27	22)	Col. 3:4, 10-11		Col. 3:5, 8-10		
929	26	19)	Col. 3:12, 14		Col. 3:12-17		
930	18	28)	Col. 3:20	1	Col. 3:20	1	128
931	2	20)	Col. 3:21	1	Col. 3:21	1	33
932	5	128)	Col. 3:24		Col. 3:22-24		
933	7	38)	Col. 4:1		Col. 4:1		
934	25	15)	Col. 4:6	1	Col. 4:2, 5-6	6	170
935	28	14)	Col. 4:17	1	Col. 4:17	1	187
15	11	(15 C.P. found in 11 Life Topics)					

NO.	LT	LOC #	CONDITIONAL PROMISES	C.P.	DOER OF THE WORD	CNDT	PG.
1 THESSALONIANS							
936	19	41)	1 Thess. 1:4, 10		1 Thess. 1:3-4		
937	5	129)	1 Thess. 2:4		1 Thess. 2:4		
938	25	29.4)	1 Thess. 2:4, 19-20		1 Thess. 2:4		
939	21	44)	1 Thess. 2:12	1	1 Thess. 2:12	1	146
940	33	9)	1 Thess. 2:13		1 Thess. 2:13		
941	22	11)	1 Thess. 4:1, 3, 7		1 Thess. 4:1-2		
942	26	20)	1 Thess. 4:6		1 Thess. 4:3-6		
943	8	45)	1 Thess. 4:9-10, 12		1 Thess. 4:9, 11		
944	16	12)	1 Thess. 4:14-15, 17		1 Thess. 4:14, 18		
945	27	23)	1 Thess. 4:14, 16	6	1 Thess. 4:14, 18	3	181
946	19	42)	1 Thess. 5:2, 4-5, 9-10		1 Thess. 5:2, 6, 8, 11		
947	5	130)	1 Thess. 5:18, 24		1 Thess. 5:13, 15		
948	6	41)	1 Thess. 5:18, 24		1 Thess. 5:16, 18		
949	12	45)	1 Thess. 5:18, 24		1 Thess. 5:14		
950	18	29)	1 Thess. 5:18, 24		1 Thess. 5:14		
951	22	12)	1 Thess. 5:18, 24		1 Thess. 5:19-22		
952	24	14)	1 Thess. 5:18, 24	3	1 Thess. 5:17	1	161
953	26	21)	1 Thess. 5:18, 24		1 Thess. 5:12-13		
18	14	(18 C.P. found in 14 Life Topics)					

NO.	LT	LOC #	CONDITIONAL PROMISES	C.P.	DOER OF THE WORD	CNDT	PG.
			2 THESSALONIANS				
954	11	40)	2 Thess. 1:5-8		2 Thess. 1:4		
955	27	24)	2 Thess. 1:10	2	2 Thess. 1:10	1	182
956	27	25)	2 Thess. 2:3-4		2 Thess. 2:2-3		
957	19	43)	2 Thess. 2:13-14		2 Thess. 2:13, 15		
4	3	(4 C.P. found in 3 Life Topics)					
			1 TIMOTHY				
958	26	22)	1 Tim. 1:4-5		1 Tim. 1:3-5		
959	32	13)	1 Tim. 1:8-11		1 Tim. 1:8		
960	7	39)	1 Tim. 1:18		1 Tim. 1:19		
961	5	131)	1 Tim. 2:2		1 Tim. 2:1-2		
962	6	42)	1 Tim. 2:15		1 Tim. 2:15		
963	28	15)	1 Tim. 3:1	2	1 Tim. 3:1-4, 6-7	18	188
964	7	40)	1 Tim. 3:13		1 Tim. 3:8-13		
965	6	43)	1 Tim. 4:4	2	1 Tim. 4:4	2	60
966	7	41)	1 Tim. 4:6, 8		1 Tim. 4:6-8, 10		
967	6	44)	1 Tim. 4:8	2	1 Tim. 4:8	2	60
968	21	45)	1 Tim. 4:10	2	1 Tim. 4:10	2	146
969	28	16)	1 Tim. 4:15, 16		1 Tim. 4:12-16		
970	18	30)	1 Tim. 4:15, 16		1 Tim. 4:12-16		
971	7	42)	1 Tim. 5:4		1 Tim. 5:1-3		
972	13	18)	1 Tim. 5:16		1 Tim. 5:16		
973	3	26)	1 Tim. 5:17, 18		1 Tim. 5:17		
974	7	43)	1 Tim. 5:17, 18		1 Tim. 5:17		
975	8	46)	1 Tim. 5:17, 18		1 Tim. 5:17		
976	26	23)	1 Tim. 5:20, 24-25		1 Tim. 5:20, 22		

NO.	LT	LOC #	CONDITIONAL PROMISES	C.P.	DOER OF THE WORD	CNDT	PG.
977	5	132)	1 Tim. 6:1		1 Tim. 6:1		
978	5	133)	1 Tim. 6:1-2		1 Tim. 6:2		
979	8	47)	1 Tim. 6:6		1 Tim. 6:6, 8, 11-12		
980	8	48)	1 Tim. 6:17-19		1 Tim. 6:17, 18		
23	11	(23 C.P. found in 11 Life Topics)					

2 TIMOTHY

NO.	LT	LOC #	CONDITIONAL PROMISES	C.P.	DOER OF THE WORD	CNDT	PG.
981	25	16)	2 Tim. 1:7, 9, 12		2 Tim. 1:8, 12		
982	15	38)	2 Tim. 1:14		2 Tim. 1:13-14		
983	17	55)	2 Tim. 2:7	1	2 Tim. 2:7	1	122
984	25	17)	2 Tim. 2:9-10	2	2 Tim. 2:10	1	171
985	19	44)	2 Tim. 2:11-13		2 Tim. 2:11-13		
986	5	134)	2 Tim. 2:19		2 Tim. 2:19		
987	31	7.4)	2 Tim. 2:20-21		2 Tim. 2:21		
988	25	18)	2 Tim. 2:25-26		2 Tim. 2:23-25		
989	15	39)	2 Tim. 3:12	2	2 Tim. 3:12	1	109
990	17	56)	2 Tim. 3:15		2 Tim. 3:15		
991	27	26)	2 Tim. 4:8	2	2 Tim. 4:8	1	182
11	8	(11 C.P. found in 8 Life Topics)					

TITUS

NO.	LT	LOC #	CONDITIONAL PROMISES	C.P.	DOER OF THE WORD	CNDT	PG.
992	7	44)	Titus 1:6, 9		Titus 1:6-9		
993	6	45)	Titus 1:15	1	Titus 1:15	1	60
994	15	40)	Titus 2:8		Titus 2:1, 7-8		
995	19	45)	Titus 2:11, 14		Titus 2:12-14		
996	21	46)	Titus 3:7-8		Titus 3:8		
997	7	45)	Titus 3:14		Titus 3:14		
6	5	(6 C.P. found in 5 Life Topics)					

NO.	LT	LOC #	CONDITIONAL PROMISES	C.P.	DOER OF THE WORD	CNDT	PG.
			PHILEMON				
998	25	19)	Philem. 6		Philem. 5-6		
I	I	(1 C.P. found in 1 Life Topics)					
			HEBREWS				
999	22	13)	Heb. 2:1		Heb. 2:1		
1000	19	46)	Heb. 3:6		Heb. 3:6		
1001	22	14)	Heb. 3:12-13		Heb. 3:12-13		
1002	19	47)	Heb. 3:14-15		Heb. 3:14-15		
1003	21	47)	Heb. 4:1, 3, 7, 10-11		Heb. 4:1, 3, 7, 10-11		
1004	23	9)	Heb. 4:16	2	Heb. 4:16	I	155
1005	28	17)	Heb. 5:4	I	Heb. 5:4	I	189
1006	22	30.4)	Heb. 5:14		Heb. 5:14		
1007	12	46)	Heb. 6:11		Heb. 6:11		
1008	19	48)	Heb. 6:11-12, 14, 18		Heb. 6:11-12, 15, 18		
1009	3	31.4)	Heb. 7:8		Heb. 7:8		
1010	8	65.4)	Heb. 7:8		Heb. 7:8		
1011	21	48)	Heb. 7:25	2	Heb. 7:25	I	146
1012	21	49)	Heb. 9:15		Heb. 9:15		
1013	27	27)	Heb. 9:28	4	Heb. 9:28	I	182
1014	19	49)	Heb. 10:34-36, 38-39		Heb. 10:34-36, 38-39		
1015	30	13)	Heb. 11:6	5	Heb. 11:6	4	197
1016	5	135)	Heb. 11:14, 16		Heb. 11:13-14, 16		
1017	19	50)	Heb. 12:2	I	Heb. 12:1-2	4	134
1018	15	41)	Heb. 12:3		Heb. 12:3		

NO.	LT	LOC #	CONDITIONAL PROMISES	C.P.	DOER OF THE WORD	CNDT	PG.
1019	9	24)	Heb. 12:6-7, 9, 11	5	Heb. 12:5, 7, 9, 11	5	78
1020	26	34.4)	Heb. 12:13		Heb. 12:12-13		
1021	5	136)	Heb. 12:14-16		Heb. 12:14-15		
1022	3	27)	Heb. 13:16	1	Heb. 13:16	2	40
1023	30	14)	Heb. 13:16	1	Heb. 13:16	2	198
1024	5	137)	Heb. 13:17		Heb. 13:17		
1025	18	31)	Heb. 13:17		Heb. 13:17		
27	15	(27 C.P. found in 15 Life Topics)					
			JAMES				
1026	15	42)	James 1:3-4	4	James 1:2-4	3	110
1027	17	57)	James 1:5	4	James 1:5-6	3	122
1028	22	15)	James 1:12		James 1:12		
1029	5	138)	James 1:18, 20-21, 25		James 1:16, 19, 21, 25		
1030	13	19)	James 1:27		James 1:27		
1031	22	16)	James 1:27		James 1:27		
1032	5	139)	James 2:5, 8		James 2:5, 8		
1033	32	14)	James 2:10, 13		James 2:10, 12		
1034	33	10)	James 2:17, 20, 22, 24, 26		James 2:17, 22, 24, 26		
1035	7	46)	James 3:1	1	James 3:1	2	65
1036	17	58)	James 3:17-18		James 3:13, 17-18		
1037	30	15)	James 4:2-6		James 4:2-4, 6		
1038	29	6)	James 4:7	1	James 4:7	2	193
1039	12	47)	James 4:8, 10		James 4:8-10		
1040	23	10)	James 4:17		James 4:17		
1041	27	28)	James 5:8	1	James 5:8	1	182

NO.	LT	LOC #	CONDITIONAL PROMISES	C.P.	DOER OF THE WORD	CNDT	PG.
1042	15	43)	James 5:11		James 5:11		
1043	26	24)	James 5:12		James 5:8-9, 12		
1044	24	15)	James 5:14-16	7	James 5:14-16	8	162
1045	9	25)	James 5:19-20	3	James 5:20	1	79
20	16	(20 C.P. found in 16 Life Topics)					
1 PETER							
1046	19	51)	1 Pet. 1:3-5		1 Pet. 1:5		
1047	12	48)	1 Pet. 1:6-7, 9		1 Pet. 1:6-9		
1048	5	140)	1 Pet. 1:13, 17-21		1 Pet. 1:13-18, 21		
1049	17	59)	1 Pet. 2:2-3	2	1 Pet. 2:1-3	7	122
1050	19	52)	1 Pet. 2:5-6, 9		1 Pet. 2:6, 9		
1051	27	29)	1 Pet. 2:12, 15		1 Pet. 2:11-13, 15-17		
1052	15	44)	1 Pet. 2:19-21		1 Pet. 2:18-21		
1053	19	53)	1 Pet. 2:24-25		1 Pet. 2:24-25		
1054	2	21)	1 Pet. 3:1-2, 4, 6		1 Pet. 3:1-4, 6		
1055	24	16)	1 Pet. 3:7	1	1 Pet. 3:7	3	162
1056	21	50)	1 Pet. 3:9		1 Pet. 3:8-9		
1057	12	49)	1 Pet. 3:10		1 Pet. 3:10-11		
1058	24	17)	1 Pet. 3:12	2	1 Pet. 3:12	2	163
1059	25	20)	1 Pet. 3:13-14, 16		1 Pet. 3:13-16		
1060	19	70.4)	1 Pet. 3:21-22		1 Pet. 3:21		
1061	22	17)	1 Pet. 4:1-2		1 Pet. 4:1-2, 6		
1062	26	25)	1 Pet. 4:8		1 Pet. 4:7-10		
1063	33	11)	1 Pet. 4:11	4	1 Pet. 4:10-11	3	213
1064	27	30)	1 Pet. 4:13		1 Pet. 4:12-13		
1065	15	45)	1 Pet. 4:14, 16-17, 19		1 Pet. 4:14-17, 19		

NO.	LT	LOC #	CONDITIONAL PROMISES	C.P.	DOER OF THE WORD	CNDT	PG.
1066	27	31)	I Pet. 5:4		I Pet. 5:2-3		
1067	18	32)	I Pet. 5:5	3	I Pet. 5:5	4	128
1068	26	26)	I Pet. 5:5-6		I Pet. 5:5-6		
1069	12	50)	I Pet. 5:7	I	I Pet. 5:7	I	96
1070	22	18)	I Pet. 5:8-9		I Pet. 5:8-9		
1071	11	41)	I Pet. 5:10		I Pet. 5:10		
1072	12	51)	I Pet. 5:10	6	I Pet. 5:10	I	97
1073	13	20)	I Pet. 5:10		I Pet. 5:10		
1074	15	46)	I Pet. 5:10		I Pet. 5:10		
1075	27	32)	I Pet. 5:10		I Pet. 5:10		
1076	6	46)	I Pet. 5:14	I	I Pet. 5:14	2	60
31	18	(31 C.P. found in 18 Life Topics)					
			2 PETER				
1077	5	158.4)	2 Pet. 1:2-4		2 Pet. 1:2-4		
1078	17	60)	2 Pet. 1:8, 10		2 Pet. 1:5-8, 10		
1079	19	71.4)	2 Pet. 1:8, 10-11		2 Pet. 1:5-8, 10		
1080	22	19)	2 Pet. 2:9	2	2 Pet. 2:9	I	151
1081	21	51)	2 Pet. 3:9	4	2 Pet. 3:9	I	147
1082	22	20)	2 Pet. 3:17		2 Pet. 3:14-15, 17-18		
6	5	(6 C.P. found in 5 Life Topics)					
			I JOHN				
1083	25	21)	I John 1:3-4		I John 1:2		
1084	19	54)	I John 1:7	2	I John 1:7	I	134
1085	26	27)	I John 1:7	2	I John 1:7	I	174
1086	23	11)	I John 1:9	4	I John 1:9	I	155
1087	19	55)	I John 2:3, 5-6		I John 2:3, 5-6		
1088	26	28)	I John 2:10	3	I John 2:10	I	175

NO.	LT	LOC #	CONDITIONAL PROMISES	C.P.	DOER OF THE WORD	CNDT	PG.
1089	19	56)	1 John 2:17, 23-25		1 John 2:17, 23-24		
1090	17	64.4)	1 John 2:27		1 John 2:27		
1091	27	33)	1 John 2:28	3	1 John 2:28	1	183
1092	19	57)	1 John 2:29	3	1 John 2:29	3	135
1093	19	58)	1 John 3:3, 6-7, 9		1 John 3:3, 6-7, 9		
1094	24	18)	1 John 3:22		1 John 3:22-23		
1095	25	22)	1 John 4:2, 4, 6	7	1 John 4:2, 6	2	171
1096	30	16)	1 John 4:7, 11	5	1 John 4:7, 11	3	198
1097	19	59)	1 John 4:12, 15-16		1 John 4:12, 15-16		
1098	11	42)	1 John 4:18	2	1 John 4:18	1	89
1099	12	52)	1 John 4:18	2	1 John 4:18	1	97
1100	13	21)	1 John 4:18		1 John 4:18		
1101	15	47)	1 John 4:18		1 John 4:18		
1102	16	13)	1 John 4:18		1 John 4:18		
1103	18	33)	1 John 4:18		1 John 4:18		
1104	25	23)	1 John 4:18		1 John 4:18		
1105	26	29)	1 John 5:1	4	1 John 5:1	2	175
1106	21	52)	1 John 5:4-5, 10, 12		1 John 5:4-5, 10, 12		
1107	24	19)	1 John 5:14-15	4	1 John 5:14-15	3	163
1108	26	30)	1 John 5:16-17		1 John 5:16		
1109	19	60)	1 John 5:18		1 John 5:18, 21		
1110	22	21)	1 John 5:18	3	1 John 5:18, 21	3	151
28	16	(28 C.P. found in 16 Life Topics)					

2 JOHN

NO.	LT	LOC #	CONDITIONAL PROMISES	C.P.	DOER OF THE WORD	CNDT	PG.
1111	12	53)	2 John 2-3		2 John 2		
1112	27	34)	2 John 8		2 John 8		

NO.	LT	LOC #	CONDITIONAL PROMISES	C.P.	DOER OF THE WORD	CNDT	PG.
1113	19	61)	2 John 9	3	2 John 9	1	134
3	3	(3 C.P. found in 3 Life Topics)					

3 JOHN							
1114	3	28)	3 John 6, 8		3 John 5-6, 8		
1115	26	31)	3 John 6, 8		3 John 5-6, 8		
1116	22	22)	3 John 11		3 John 11		
1117	30	17)	3 John 11	2	3 John 11	2	198
4	4	(4 C.P. found in 4 Life Topics)					

REVELATION							
1118	17	61)	Rev. 1:3	3	Rev. 1:3	3	123
1119	21	53)	Rev. 2:7		Rev. 2:2-7		
1120	16	14)	Rev. 2:10-11		Rev. 2:10-11		
1121	23	14.4)	Rev. 2:17		Rev. 2:16-17		
1122	27	35)	Rev. 2:23, 26-29		Rev. 2:19, 25-26, 29		
1123	19	62)	Rev. 3:5-6		Rev. 3:2-3, 5-6		
1124	27	36)	Rev. 3:8-13		Rev. 3:8, 10-13		
1125	21	54)	Rev. 3:18-22		Rev. 3:18-22		
1126	22	23)	Rev. 12:11; 13:9-10		Rev. 12:11-12, 17; 13:9-10		
1127	15	48)	Rev. 14:12		Rev. 14:12		
1128	16	15)	Rev. 14:13	3	Rev. 14:13	1	115
1129	15	53.4)	Rev. 16:15		Rev. 16:15		
1130	27	37)	Rev. 20:6		Rev. 20:6		
1131	21	55)	Rev. 21:6		Rev. 21:6		
1132	11	43)	Rev. 21:7	4	Rev. 21:7	1	89
1133	27	38)	Rev. 22:7, 14		Rev. 22:7, 14		
16	9	(28 C.P. found in 16 Life Topics)					

Reflection Notes

Reflection Notes

Reflection Notes